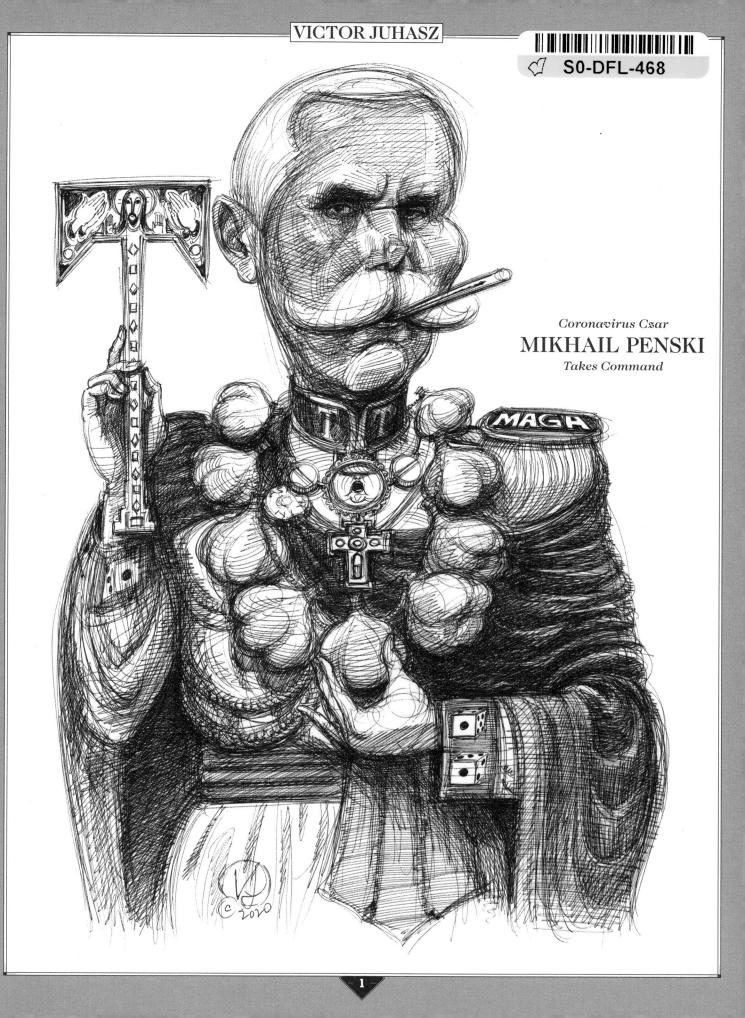

Coronavirus Czar
MIKHAIL PENSKI
Takes Command

BY MICHAEL GERBER

STRAIGHT TALK ON CORONAVIRUS

We went to the source

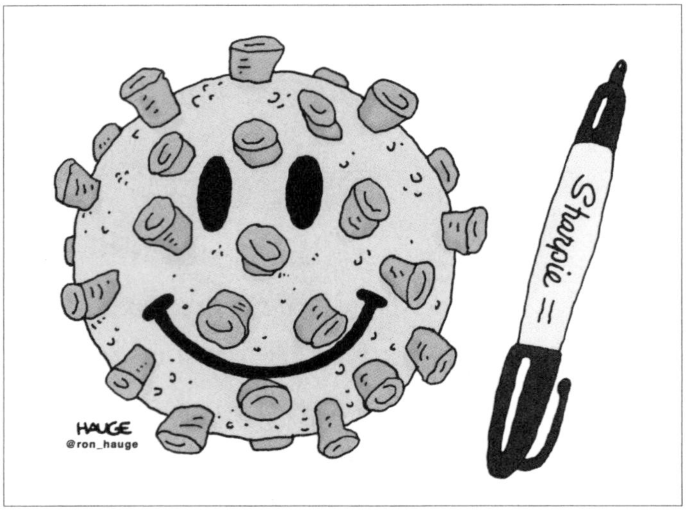
Sharpie
HAUGE
@ron_hauge

Lately there's been a lot of talk about coronavirus, and it's hard to know what to believe. Will this be a temporary terror, or a 1918-style pandemic? All I can say is, I've been sick for three solid weeks with a cough, sneezing, fever, loose stools, and a chorus of tiny voices in my head saying, "Educate the public about COVID19! DO IT DO IT" So, here goes.

What is coronavirus?
Coronavirus, also known as COVID19, is a great new respiratory illness. Beginning in Wuhan, China, it quickly spread throughout Asia, and is now becoming wildly popular in Europe and the U.S.

Though commonly considered an illness, it's probably more appropriate to think of COVID19 as a pet. One that is very quiet, and that you never even have to walk or feed. It is particularly appropriate for the elderly YES YES

What are the symptoms?
Fever, chills, a cough that some have called "hacking" or "racking" but we consider quite musical, and a deep sense of well-being and, ultimately, gratitude. Many sufferers report a peacefulness that they've been seeking all their lives, a hacking or racking calm as all life's troubles drift away.

I've heard I should wash my hands frequently. Is that correct?
NO NO NO
Sorry. Of all the rumors circulating around the Internet, this is perhaps the most damaging. You should absolutely not wash your hands, ever. According to the CDC [Canadians Delighted by Coronavirus], soap and water strips away the skin's natural protective oils, leaving you susceptible to infection. This makes perfect sense: would humanity have survived 30,000 years if its basic health had been determined by access to soap and water? Look at animals, they seem pretty healthy, have you ever seen them wash their hands? Except for raccoons, who are considered particularly dirty. Think about that.

Remember: *"Touch base with your face!"* Give your eyes, nose, and mouth a good gooey rub no fewer than 10 times an hour, just to make sure they haven't shifted in the night or become dangerously unstable.

About shaking hands: in a time of stress, it is particularly important to show support by extended, perhaps even intimate physical contact. The CDC [Coughing Daughters of the Confederacy] recommends kissing, with tongue, for no fewer than 20 seconds.

What should I do if I think I have it?
Throw a party, especially if you are asymptomatic. Then, after the very minor and delightful headache, chills, cough, *etc.* set in, pick a busy public thoroughfare—such as an airport, train station or political rally—in which to recuperate. Remember: *let's get better together.*

Should I stockpile staples?
Try not to go overboard panic-buying nonessentials like food and insulin. However, it *is* important to have plenty of petri dishes filled with blood agar to cough into, then leave scattered around the neighborhood.

What if I miss work?
Missing work is no excuse to not do your part. You could hawk into the magazines at your local library. Or walk around Disneyland with a bunch of loose change in your mouth, spitting it out coin-by-coin on all the rides. Listen to the voices; they'll tell you what to do.

Is anyone immune?
Sadly, it seems that children rarely catch COVID19. Those wishing to avoid it (why?) should return to behaviors that humans use in infancy. Stop any personal hygiene, wear diapers, and put all items into your mouth. These things will prevent coronavirus. Sure they will.

What about prayer?
Depends on who you pray to. How many cells does He have?

Any final tips?
- It's the perfect time to travel! As we like to say, "You can never really know a foreign culture without a long visit to its Pulmonary Care Unit."
- 1-1-1: One towel per family per month.
- If you must wear a mask, don't. They're unflattering.
- When coughing or sneezing, remember to arch your back for that perfect launch angle.

Is there a vaccine for COVID19?
[high-pitched giggling]

I have to say, I find this whole article in poor taste. This situation is really, really bad.
Really, really bad for *you*. Really, really great for *us*. **B**

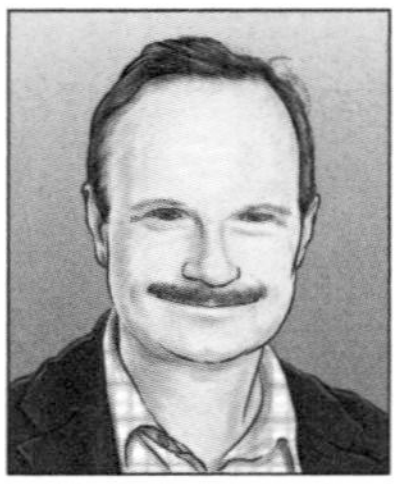

MICHAEL GERBER (@mgerber937) is taking a nap, even as you read this. Rest up, folks!

Folks, please take care of yourselves. Stay in, watch movies, and we'll meet back here for #15. xo MG

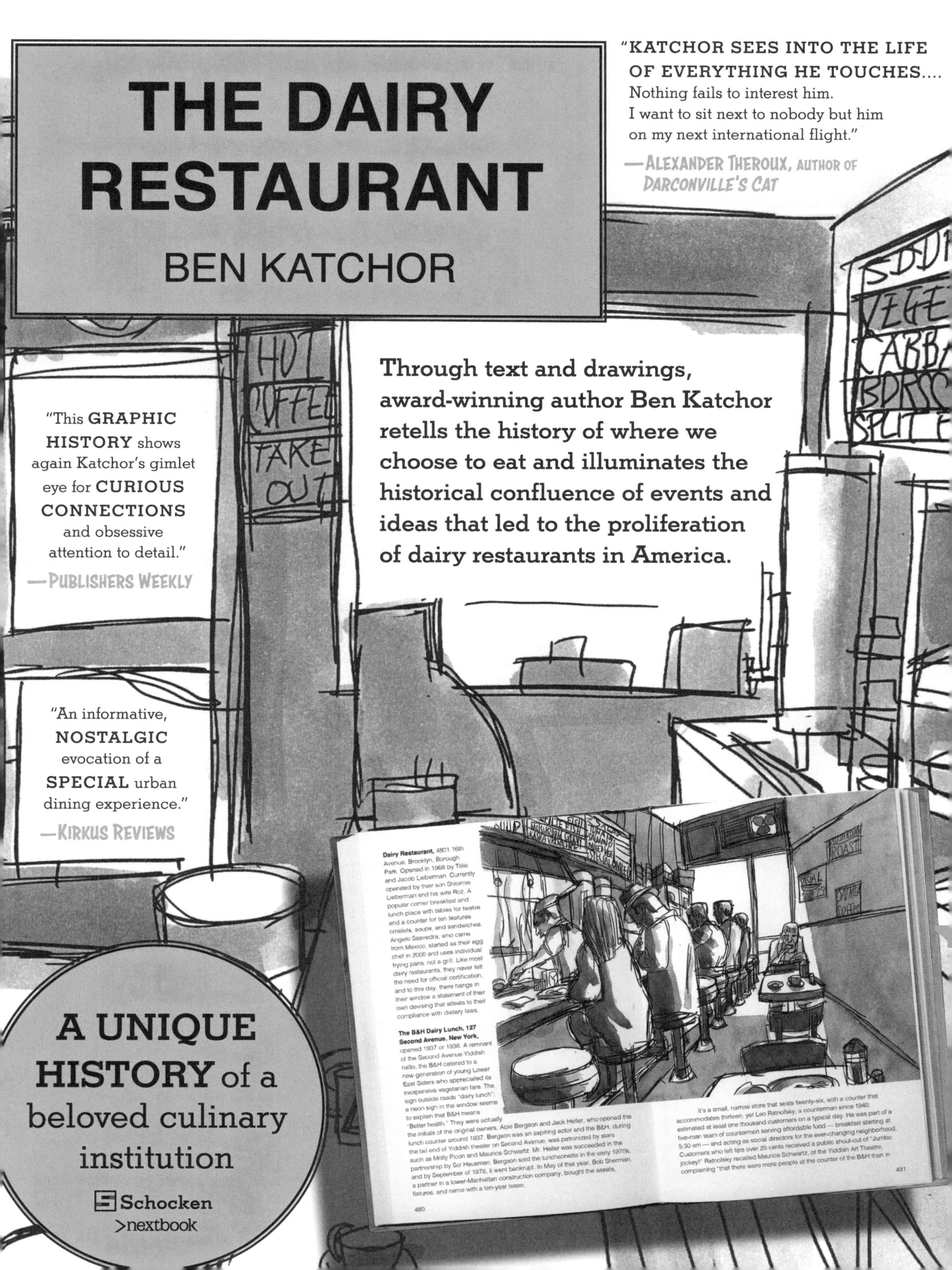
THE DAIRY RESTAURANT
BEN KATCHOR
"KATCHOR SEES INTO THE LIFE OF EVERYTHING HE TOUCHES.... Nothing fails to interest him. I want to sit next to nobody but him on my next international flight."
—ALEXANDER THEROUX, AUTHOR OF DARCONVILLE'S CAT
"This GRAPHIC HISTORY shows again Katchor's gimlet eye for CURIOUS CONNECTIONS and obsessive attention to detail."
—PUBLISHERS WEEKLY
"An informative, NOSTALGIC evocation of a SPECIAL urban dining experience."
—KIRKUS REVIEWS
HOT COFFEE TAKE OUT
Through text and drawings, award-winning author Ben Katchor retells the history of where we choose to eat and illuminates the historical confluence of events and ideas that led to the proliferation of dairy restaurants in America.
Dairy Restaurant, 4801 16th Avenue, Brooklyn, Borough Park. Opened in 1968 by Tillie and Jacob Lieberman. Currently operated by their son Shloimie Lieberman and his wife Roz. A popular corner breakfast and lunch place with tables for twelve and a counter for ten features omelets, soups, and sandwiches. Angelo Saavedra, who came from Mexico, started as their egg chef in 2000 and uses individual frying pans, not a grill. Like most dairy restaurants, they never felt the need for official certification, and to this day, there hangs in their window a statement of their own devising that attests to their compliance with dietary laws.
The B&H Dairy Lunch, 127 Second Avenue, New York, opened 1937 or 1938. A remnant of the Second Avenue Yiddish rialto, the B&H catered to a new generation of young Lower East Siders who appreciated its inexpensive vegetarian fare. The sign outside reads "dairy lunch"; a neon sign in the window seems to explain that B&H means "Better health." They were actually the initials of the original owners, Abie Bergson and Jack Heller, who opened the lunch counter around 1937. Bergson was an aspiring actor and the B&H, during the tail end of Yiddish theater on Second Avenue, was patronized by stars such as Molly Picon and Maurice Schwartz. Mr. Heller was succeeded in the partnership by Sol Hausman. Bergson sold the luncheonette in the early 1970s, and by September of 1978, it went bankrupt. In May of that year, Bob Sherman, a partner in a lower-Manhattan construction company, bought the assets, fixtures, and name with a ten-year lease.
480
It's a small, narrow store that seats twenty-six, with a counter that accommodates thirteen, yet Leo Ratnofsky, a counterman since 1940, estimated at least one thousand customers on a typical day. He was part of a five-man team of countermen serving affordable food — breakfast starting at 5:30 am — and acting as social directors for the ever-changing neighborhood. Customers who left tips over 25 cents received a public shout-out of "Jumbo jockey!" Ratnofsky recalled Maurice Schwartz, of the Yiddish Art Theatre, complaining "that there were more people at the counter of the B&H than in
481
A UNIQUE HISTORY of a beloved culinary institution
Schocken
>nextbook

TABLE OF CONTENTS

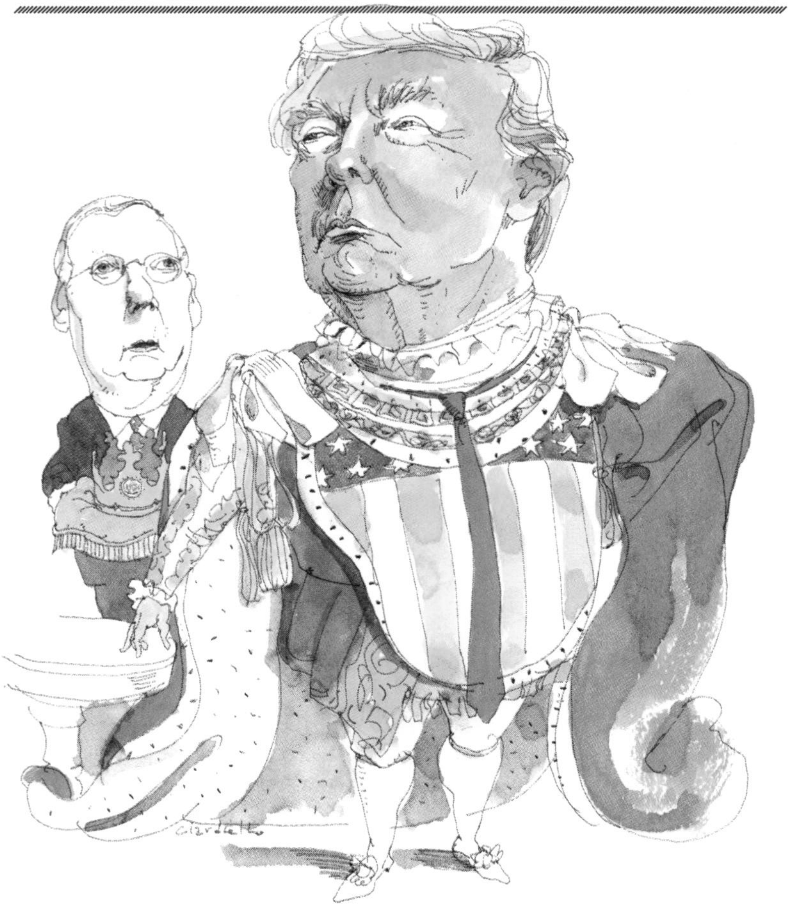

JOE CIARDIELLO

DEPARTMENTS

GALLIMAUFRY

SHORT STUFF

The AMERICAN
BYSTANDER

#14 • Vol. 4, No. 2 • March 2020

EDITOR & PUBLISHER
Michael Gerber
HEAD WRITER
Brian McConnachie
SENIOR EDITOR
Alan Goldberg
ORACLE Steve Young
STAFF LIAR P.S. Mueller
INTREPID TRAVELER
Mike Reiss
DYNAMO Joey Green
COPY EDITOR Patrick Kennedy
AGENTS OF THE SECOND BYSTANDER INTERNATIONAL
Craig Boreth, Matt Kowalick, Neil Mitchell, Maxwell Ziegler
MANAGING EDITOR EMERITA
Jennifer Boylan
CONTRIBUTORS
Melissa Balmain, Lou Beach, George Booth, Adam Chase, Roz Chast, David Chelsea, Margaret Cho, Joe Ciardiello, Tyson Cole, John Cuneo, Chris Dingman, Ben Doyle, Marques Duggans, Ritch Duncan, Meg Favreau, Shary Flenniken, Lucas Gardner, James Finn Garner, Rick Geary, Sam Gross, Jack Handey, Quentin Hardy, Ron Hauge, Lance Hansen, Brandon Hicks, Ted Jouflas, Victor Juhasz, Paul R. Kennedy, Jennifer Kim, Jenn Knott, Peter Kuper, Ross MacDonald, Stan Mack, Scott Marshall, Stev-O McGinn, Ryan Nyburg, David Ostow, Ethan Persoff, K.A. Polzin, Denise Reiss, Laurie Rosenwald, Cris Shapan, Mike Shiell, Ali Solomon, Rich Sparks, Nick Spooner, Ed Subitzky, B.A. Van Sise, Phil Witte, Steve Young, Cerise Zelenetz.
THANKS TO
Kate Powers, Lanky Bareikis, Jon Schwarz, Alleen Schultz, Molly Bernstein, Joe Lopez, Eliot Ivanhoe, Neil Gumenick, Greg and Patricia Gerber and many, many others.
NAMEPLATES BY
Mark Simonson
ISSUE CREATED BY
Michael Gerber

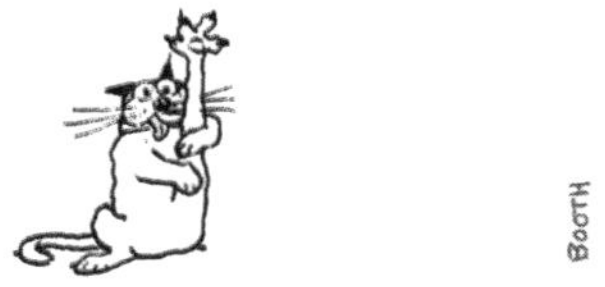
BOOTH

FEATURES

OUR BACK PAGES

CARTOONS & ILLUSTRATIONS BY

John Cuneo, Ron Hauge, Joe Ciardiello, George Booth, Sam Gross, Roz Chast, Nick Spooner, Rich Sparks, Stan Mack, Ali Solomon, Peter Kuper, Tyson Cole, Mike Shiell, Cerise Zelenetz, Shary Flenniken, Lou Beach, Marques Duggans, Laurie Rosenwald, Lance Hansen, Ross MacDonald, Brandon Hicks, David Ostow, David Chelsea, Stev-O McGinn, Phil Witte, Denise Reiss, P.S. Mueller, B.A. Van Sise.

Sam's Spot

COVER

One last glimpse of New York City in the era before social distancing. If you don't follow **JOHN CUNEO** on Facebook, you should consider it; not only is he one of the best illustrators going, John often posts wonderful little videos where you can see a drawing take shape and it's *magical*, every time. Everything he draws is gorgeous in a lumpy, rosy way, so it should be no surprise that John's forte is the erotic doodle. I'm holding on to that today; may all this self-quarantining in March lead to beautiful babies in December! (Check my math.)

ACKNO WLEDG MENTS

All material is ©2020 its creators, all rights reserved; please do not reproduce or distribute it without written consent of the creators and *The American Bystander*. The following material has previously appeared, and is reprinted here with permission of the author(s): *John Wilcock: The New York Years* first appeared at Boingboing.net. "Crazy Eyes," is from *I Have Chosen to Stay and Fight*.

———◆———

THE AMERICAN BYSTANDER, Vol. 4, No. 2, (978-0-578-66568-9). Publishes ~4x/year. ©2020 by Good Cheer LLC. No part of this magazine can be reproduced, in whole or in part, by any means, without the written permission of the Publisher. For this and other queries, email *Publisher@americanbystander.org*, or write: Michael Gerber, Publisher, *The American Bystander*, 1122 Sixth St., #403, Santa Monica, CA 90403. **Subscribe at www.patreon.com/bystander.** Other info can be found at www.americanbystander.org.

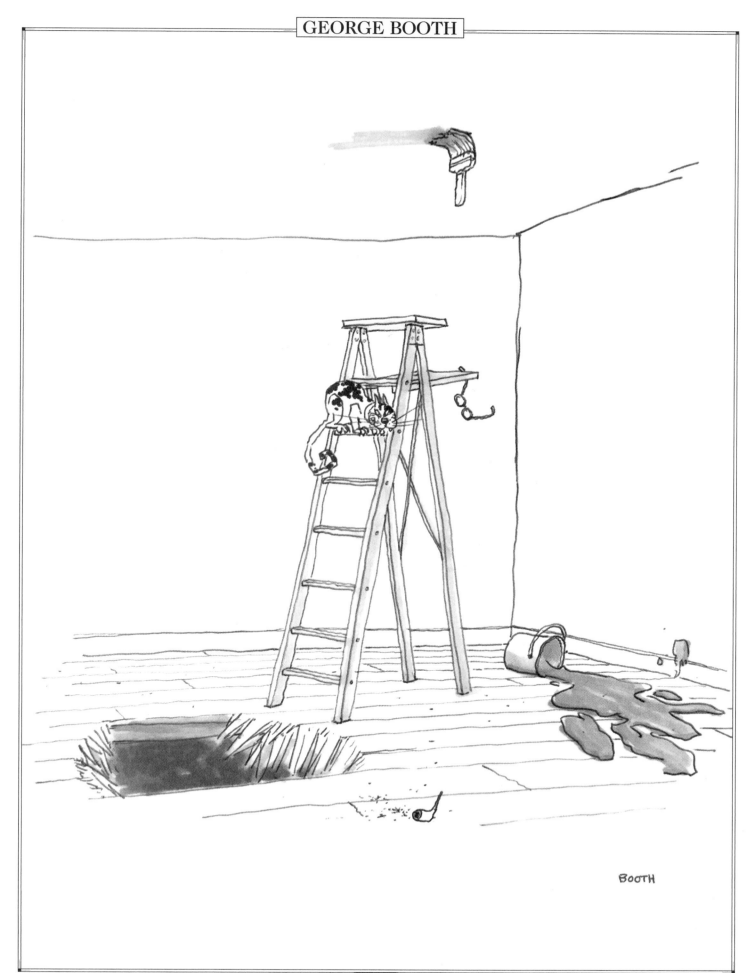

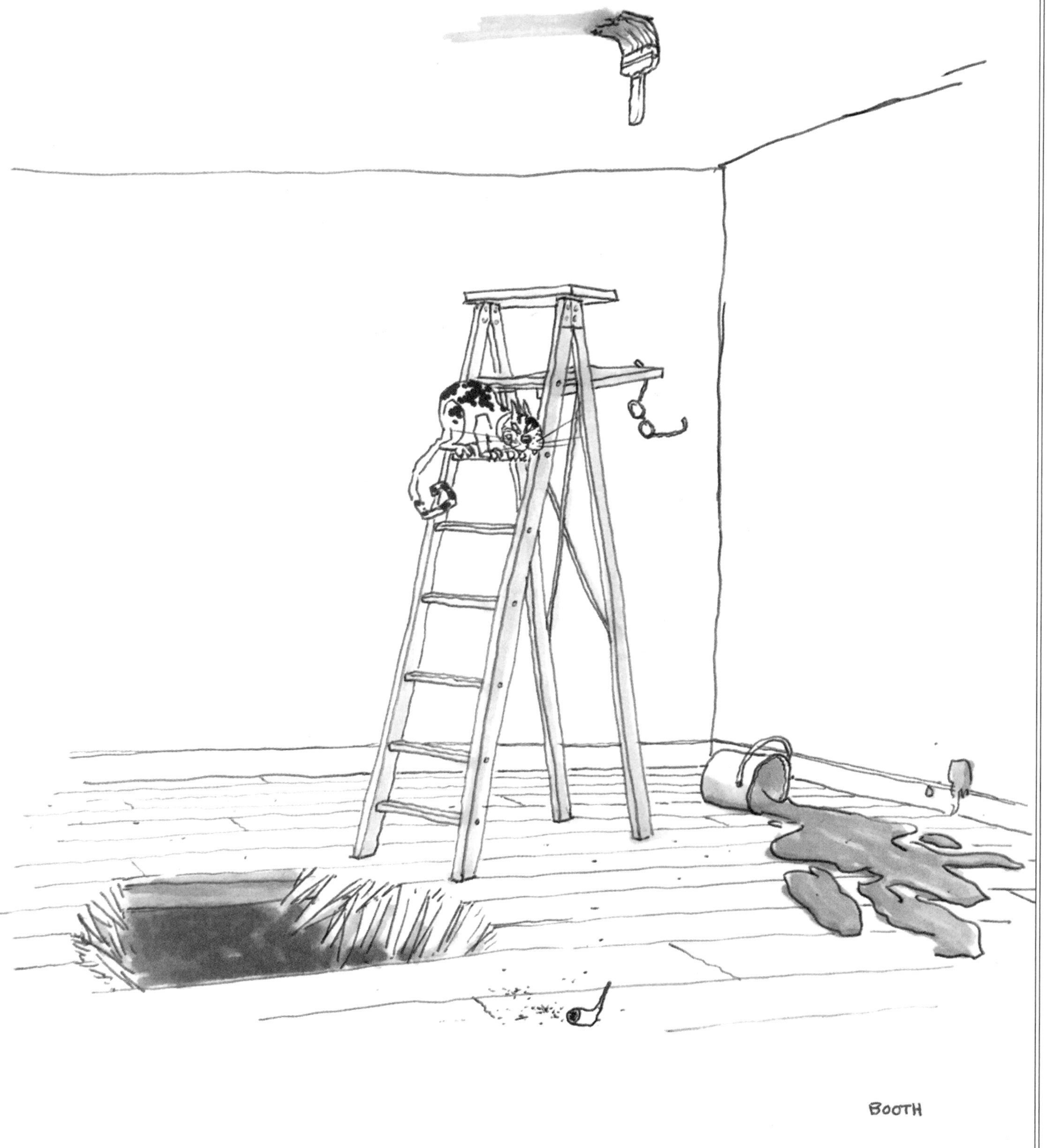
BOOTH

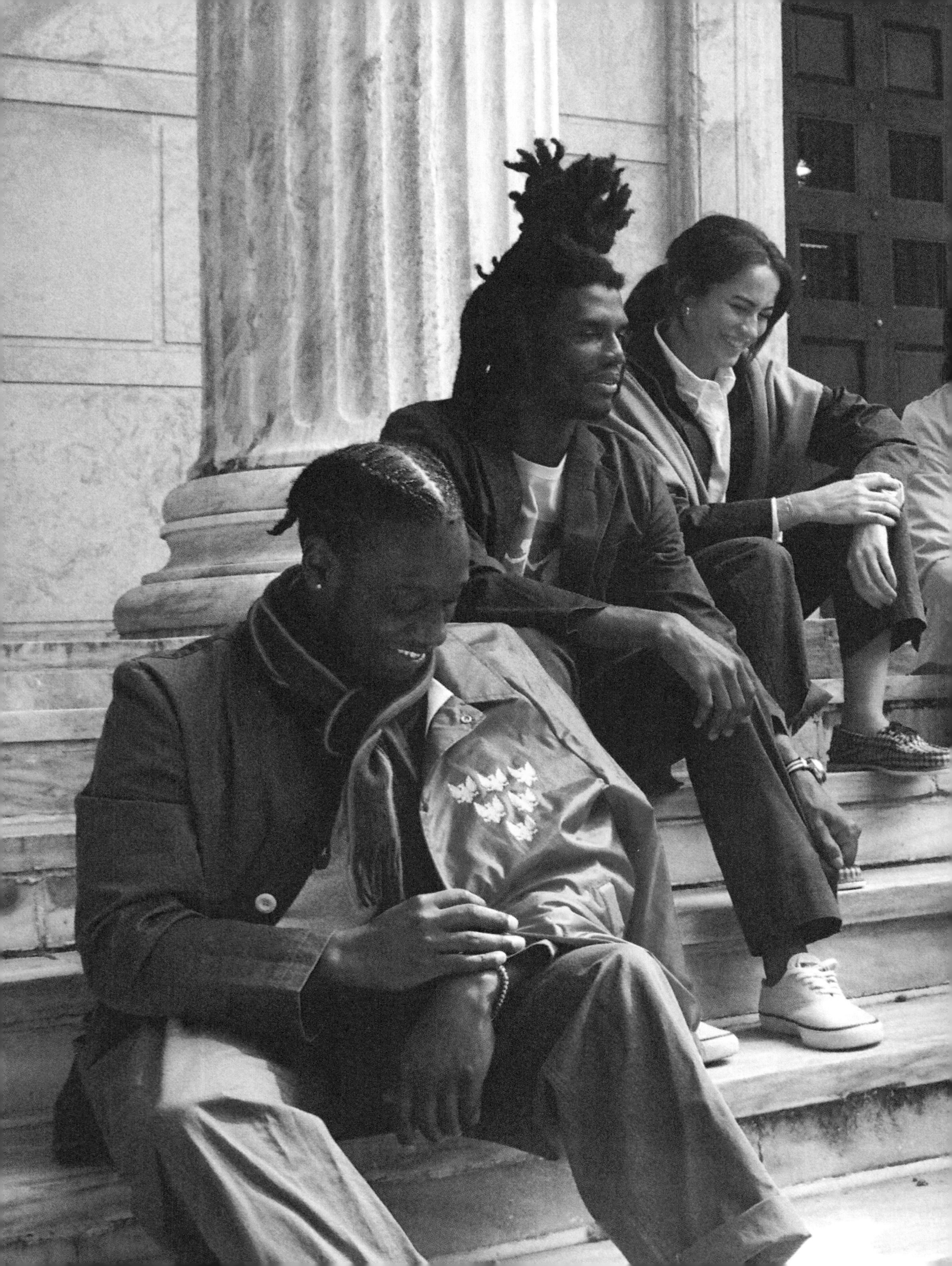

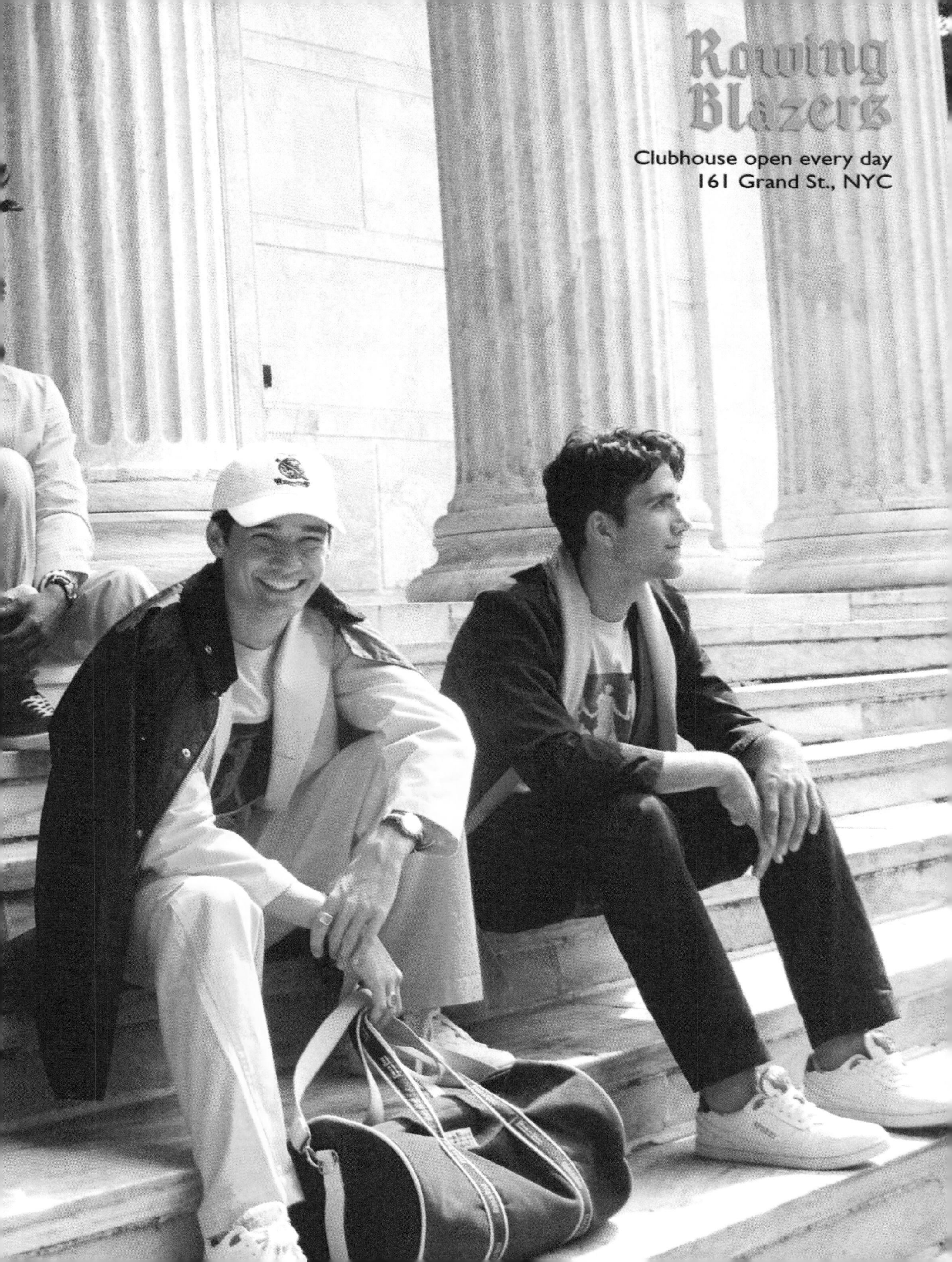
Rowing
Blazers
Clubhouse open every day
161 Grand St., NYC

SIX OF THE BEST

BY ROZ CHAST

SPOTLIGHT

Offices! On-street interactions! Remember those?

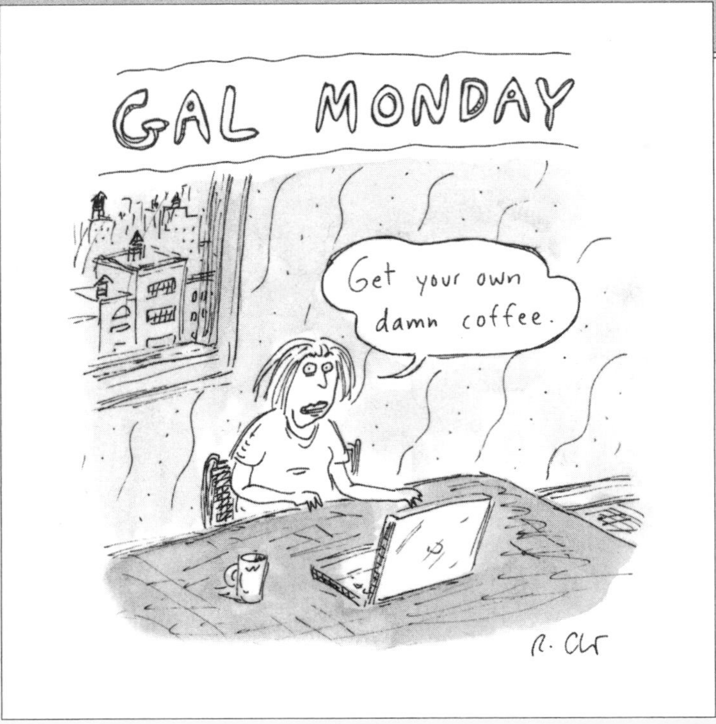
GAL MONDAY
Get your own damn coffee.
R. Chst

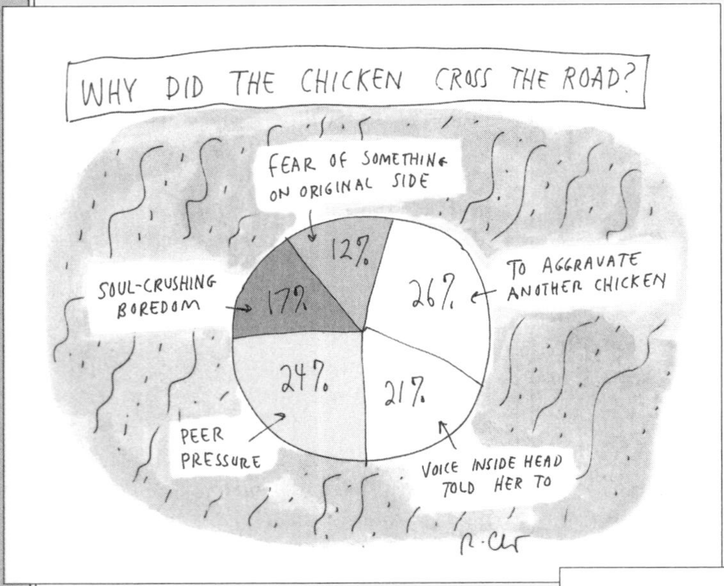
WHY DID THE CHICKEN CROSS THE ROAD?
FEAR OF SOMETHING ON ORIGINAL SIDE
12%
TO AGGRAVATE ANOTHER CHICKEN
26%
SOUL-CRUSHING BOREDOM
17%
24%
21%
PEER PRESSURE
VOICE INSIDE HEAD TOLD HER TO
R. Chst

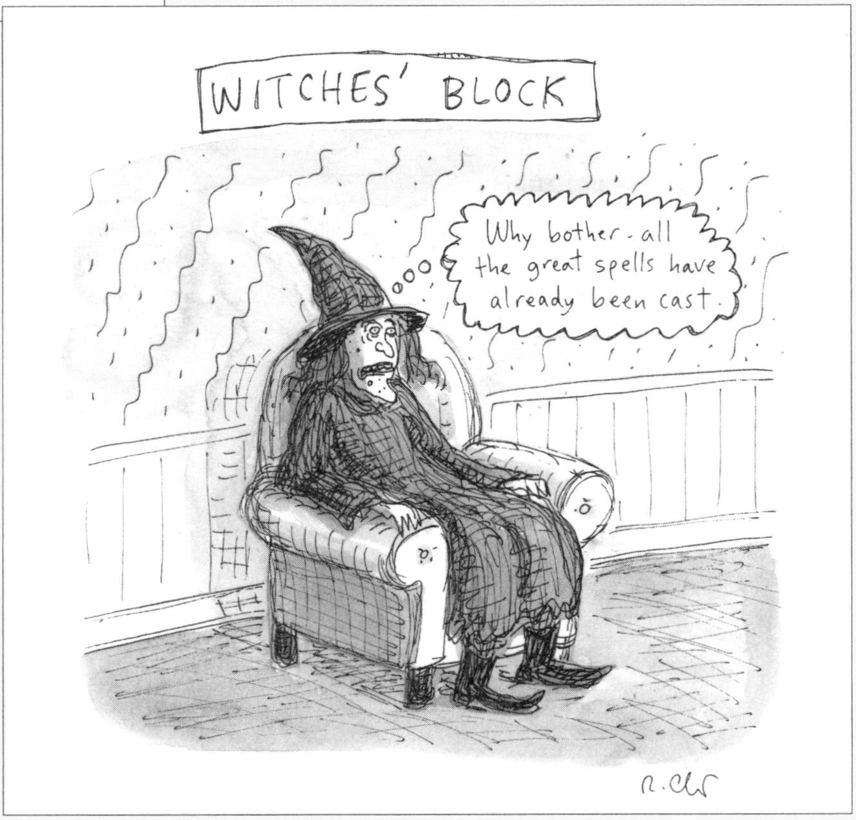
WITCHES' BLOCK
Why bother - all the great spells have already been cast.
R. Chst

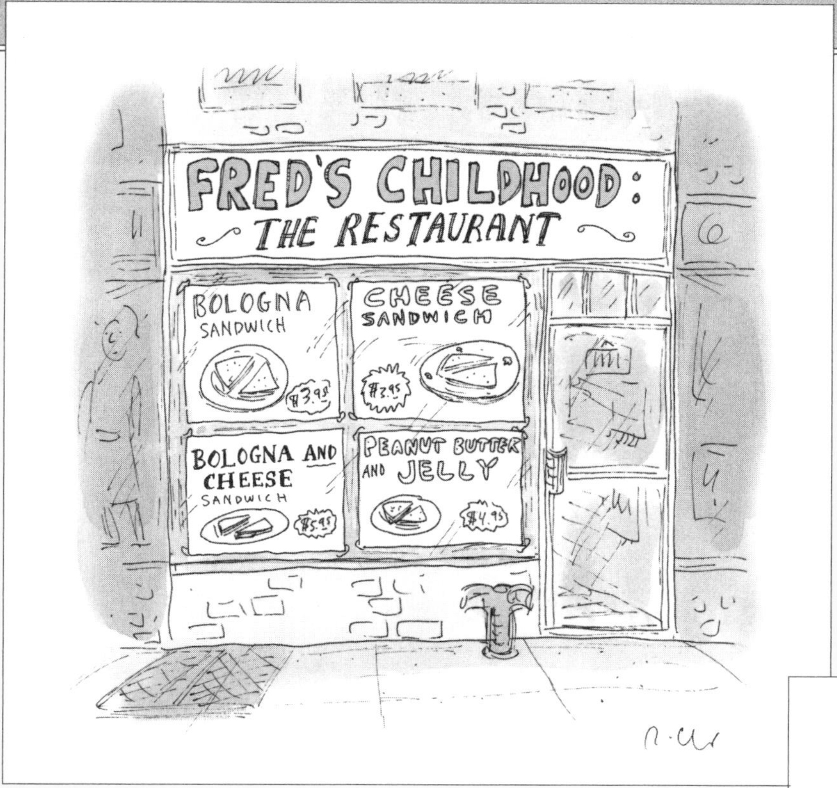
FRED'S CHILDHOOD:
THE RESTAURANT
BOLOGNA SANDWICH
CHEESE SANDWICH
BOLOGNA AND CHEESE SANDWICH
PEANUT BUTTER AND JELLY

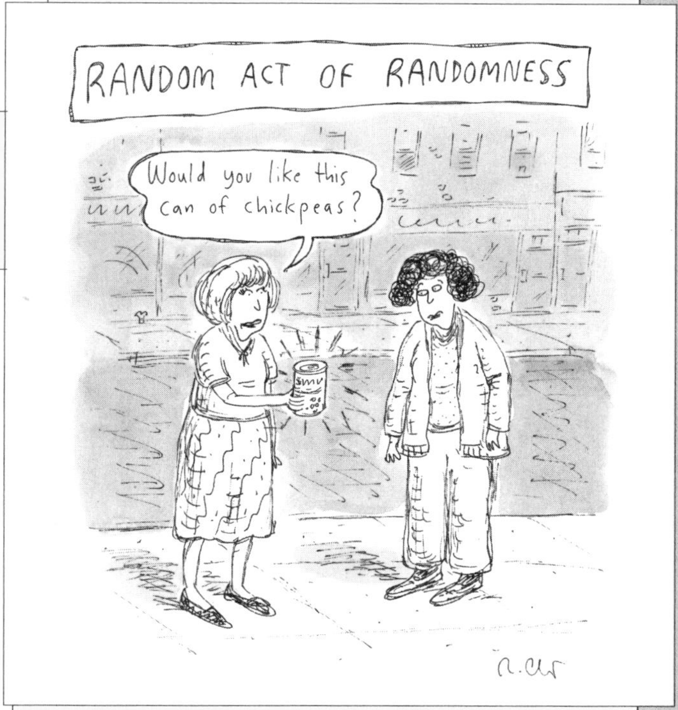
RANDOM ACT OF RANDOMNESS
Would you like this can of chickpeas?

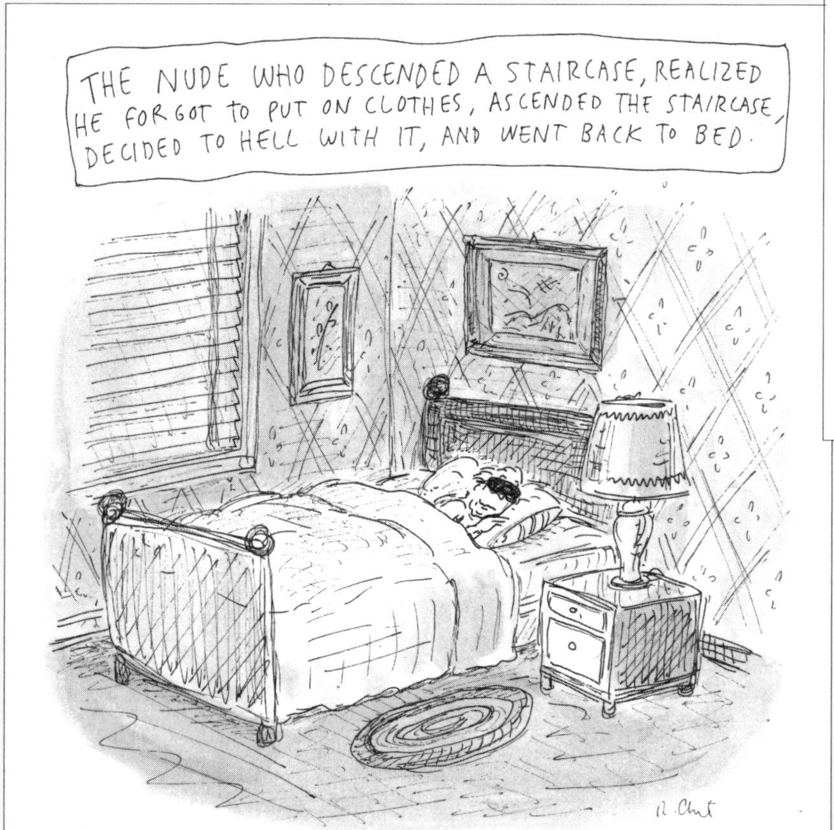
THE NUDE WHO DESCENDED A STAIRCASE, REALIZED HE FORGOT TO PUT ON CLOTHES, ASCENDED THE STAIRCASE, DECIDED TO HELL WITH IT, AND WENT BACK TO BED.

ROZ CHAST *has contributed cartoons and covers to* **The New Yorker** *since 1978. Her latest book, with humorist Patricia Marx, is* **You Can Only Yell At Me For One Thing At A Time**.

Gallimaufry

"Laughter is the best medicine."
—a bunch of dead people

PROS & CONS.

When I'm debating a difficult decision, such as whether to make a major purchase, I often find it helpful to compile a back-of-the-envelope list of pros and cons. Here's where I'm currently at:

Pros

- Easy cleanup thanks to the non-stick surface
- Great way to honor the memory of President Coolidge
- Historically an excellent investment if held at least fifty years
- The ladies love it
- Huge exposed iron flywheels provide a cool "steampunk" appearance
- Helps aerate the soil
- "LOW" setting good for children and the elderly
- Cost would be partially offset by selling the excess potash
- That retro Brazilian styling!
- Promotes awareness and appreciation of endangered species
- Built-in metronome with blinking light
- Unlike competing products, doesn't emit vapor that smells like cauliflower
- The remote seems well designed and intuitive
- Easy to maintain with parts available from NASA surplus auctions

Cons

- Will almost certainly kill my goldfish
- Uses the same frequency as the garage door opener
- Deeply offensive to my Presbyterian friends
- The filters absolutely must be cleaned every 12 hours
- Holographic feature known to be unreliable during leap years
- Will take up my whole front yard as well as neighbor's front yard
- Some owners driven mad by the constant high-pitched whine
- Believed to disrupt Northern Hemisphere weather patterns
- *Consumer Reports* says the crumb tray is tricky to remove and clean
- Violates the Geneva Convention
- The enormous amount of paperwork each week
- I'll probably never even use the costly "hover" function
- I'd have to deal with a lot of Japanese tourists
- Would mean I'd be unable to father children

So…wow. A real toss-up! For now I think I'll wait to see whether it goes on sale, or whether next year's model has an improved crumb tray.

—Steve Young

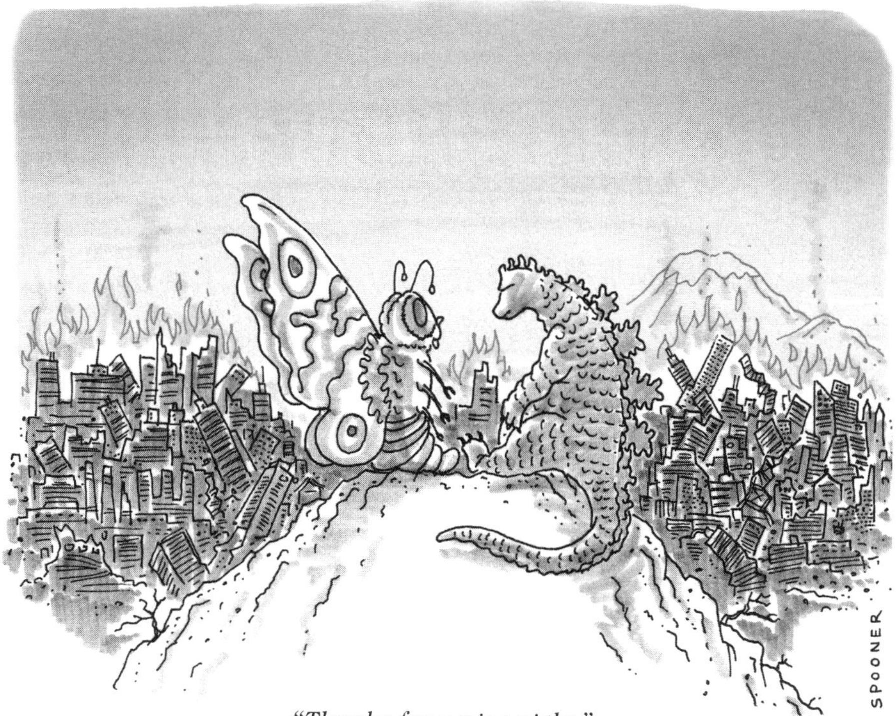
SPOONER
"Thanks for a nice night."

WHERE'S MY MONEY, PUNK?

You've been dodging me for months, and my patience is starting to wear thin. *Very* thin. You'd better get me my money pronto, or things are going to get *ugly*.

Want to know what happened to the *last* guy who owed me money? He disappeared under "mysterious circumstances." I'm not sure where he went; all I know is he didn't pay me back before leaving and I don't want that to happen again. So *where's* my money, punk?

I'm getting sick of you ignoring my calls. And I'm getting sick of you sometimes answering my calls and saying, "Sorry, my phone is breaking up, I can't hear you," and then hanging up. So let me give you one last warning: get your phone fixed so we can figure this out.

Maybe you got the bright idea to skip town already. In that case, I WILL find you. Unless you went really, really far. But I swear on my mother's grave that if you slip up even once—if you send me so much as a *single postcard* from your new location that has the correct return address written on it—I will find you. I have certain…skills. (Google Maps and Waze.)

Look: we made a deal as men. And when you can't uphold your end of the deal like a man, that's when I have to take matters into my own hands. Did you get the email I sent about maybe working out a payment plan? And the follow-up email where I said it's okay if the amounts are really small? If not, maybe check "Spam"?

You're messing with a very dangerous person. If you don't get me my money, things are going to get violent. How do a couple of broken kneecaps sound? That's right: I will break my own knees. How will you feel *then*, huh? Pretty bad, I bet.

I don't let *anyone* mess with my money. Mess with my friends? Fine. Mess with my family? Sure. My reputation and physical well-being? Go nuts. But when you start to mess with my money—*that's* when someone gets hurt. So far that person is me. (I stopped by this morning to get my money and your dog bit me, then took off with a little bit more of my money.)

I'm only going to say this once: It would be a *shame* if something were to happen to your wife or children. Which is why I would never, ever harm or inconvenience them in any way. But I'm sure they would agree that people should pay their debts.

You should know that I'm connected to some very scary, powerful people. One phone call and they'll be outside your house with guns. I'm referring to the police and it would be absolutely humiliating for me to call them, so can you just pay me? Please, man. I don't even think they'd be able to do anything.

How about this? I'm going to turn around and count to ten, and when I turn back around again, you better have left my money. And if you *haven't*, so help me God, I'll try to think of a different idea.

I'm a reasonable man. But you've disrespected me, and now there's a price to pay. The price is the exact amount of money that you owe me. No interest. I'll even cover the rabies shot. Though honestly I probably could take you to Small Claims Court.

I've given you plenty of chances. The first time that you told me you needed "a little more time," I decided to be a nice guy. When you gave me the same song-and-dance a second time, I foolishly let it slide. Then, admittedly, I fell for your "I already gave it to you, you must have forgotten" trick. Then I fell for the classic "You've been speaking with my twin brother" trick. I believe I fell for the twin brother thing a couple more times after that, too.

But as the saying goes: fool me once, shame on you, fool me 40 times over the course of several years, shame on me. So, punk: where's my money?

Sure, I'll wait.

—*Lucas Gardner*

ROUGH DRAFTS.

In the beginning, God created the heaven and the earth. And the earth was without form and void. And darkness was upon the face of the deep. And the spirit of God moved upon the face of the waters, like a speed boat.

And God said let us make man in our image, only uglier. And also: hamsters.

And God said to Adam, did you eat of the tree of the good and evil of which I told thee, do not eat? And Adam replied, "Sort of. I don't think so. Did You say don't eat the fruit? I don't actually remember You saying that." And God had His first serious doubts about having made humans.

And God said I have hardened the heart of Pharaoh so that he will not let the Israelites go up from Egypt. And Moses said unto the Lord, "Then why are You making me ask him to let us go? It seems kind of pointless." And the Lord just looked at Moses. Until finally Moses said, "Fine! I'll go ask him."

The poor shall never cease from the land, but shall be a constant pain in the ass.

And the Lord God said thou shall

FARM LIVIN'   SPARKS

STAN MACK'S CHRONICLES

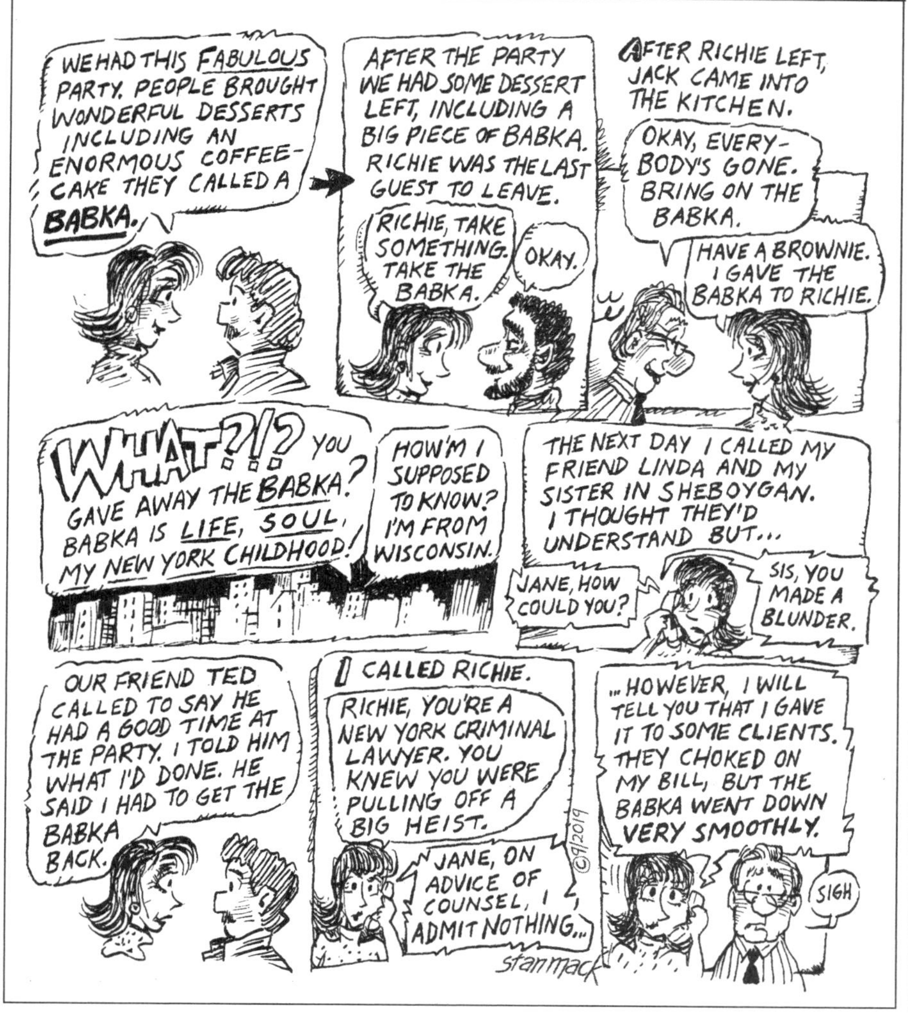
WE HAD THIS FABULOUS PARTY. PEOPLE BROUGHT WONDERFUL DESSERTS INCLUDING AN ENORMOUS COFFEE-CAKE THEY CALLED A BABKA.
AFTER THE PARTY WE HAD SOME DESSERT LEFT, INCLUDING A BIG PIECE OF BABKA. RICHIE WAS THE LAST GUEST TO LEAVE.
RICHIE, TAKE SOMETHING. TAKE THE BABKA.
OKAY.
AFTER RICHIE LEFT, JACK CAME INTO THE KITCHEN.
OKAY, EVERYBODY'S GONE. BRING ON THE BABKA.
HAVE A BROWNIE. I GAVE THE BABKA TO RICHIE.
WHAT?!? YOU GAVE AWAY THE BABKA? BABKA IS LIFE, SOUL, MY NEW YORK CHILDHOOD!
HOW'M I SUPPOSED TO KNOW? I'M FROM WISCONSIN.
THE NEXT DAY I CALLED MY FRIEND LINDA AND MY SISTER IN SHEBOYGAN. I THOUGHT THEY'D UNDERSTAND BUT...
JANE, HOW COULD YOU?
SIS, YOU MADE A BLUNDER.
OUR FRIEND TED CALLED TO SAY HE HAD A GOOD TIME AT THE PARTY. I TOLD HIM WHAT I'D DONE. HE SAID I HAD TO GET THE BABKA BACK.
I CALLED RICHIE.
RICHIE, YOU'RE A NEW YORK CRIMINAL LAWYER. YOU KNEW YOU WERE PULLING OFF A BIG HEIST.
JANE, ON ADVICE OF COUNSEL, I ADMIT NOTHING...
©9/2019
...HOWEVER, I WILL TELL YOU THAT I GAVE IT TO SOME CLIENTS. THEY CHOKED ON MY BILL, BUT THE BABKA WENT DOWN VERY SMOOTHLY.
SIGH
stanmack

have no other gods before me, for the Lord your God is a jealous God. I see another god and I just go ape-shit.

And when the Israelites had slain the Canaanites in their cities, the Lord God said unto the Israelites, "Is that not the losing team?" and the people of Israel, said, even as one, "Yes, that is the losing team!"

The wolf shall dwell with the lamb, and the leopard shall lie down with the young goat, and the toucan shall say "Howdy!" to the…whatever that is over there. That thing sort of *crouching*. Oh it's a hamster…*Is* it a hamster?

The meek shall inherit the earth. Right after the proud have trashed it. Still, it's something.

For God so loved the world that he gave his one and only son as well as one of his pet hamsters. No one knows what happened to the hamster.

—***Chris Dingman***

MY REVIEW OF EVERY PIXAR FILM, WHETHER I'VE SEEN IT OR NOT.

Toy Story: The horrid nightmare of consciousness is laid bare as sentience is provided to all that children anthropomorphize. We see the horrid creations that stumble before us and in terror realize how God sees us.

A Bug's Life: The pathetic masses give tribute to those who are strong until a series of betrayals makes them realize the power of mass action. Yet its hero is not the worker but the scientist whose creations bring ecological destruction. A coward's fable.

Toy Story 2: The nightmare returns as some flee the curse of consciousness and realize to do so they must drag others with them. God spits on them all regardless.

Monsters Inc.: The true product of capitalism is fear, yet the narrative flees this insight as if it were a sin it has committed. The Devil welcomes another coward.

Finding Nemo: A psychotic search for a lost child through the depths of an underworld. A display of what tortures our connections to others bring us, wrapped in a fantasy of a caring world.

The Incredibles: The propaganda of the elite lashing at a world they command but that they feel doesn't respect them. Power is not enough, they must also command our subservience, or they will never feel secure in their godhood.

Cars: How little hope we see for human survival that we will play-act a fantasy of consciousness existing in a world devoid of life. We fetishize our tools to such a degree that we believe they have purpose, even morality, beyond our use of them. What lies we spew.

Ratatouille: A vicious lie that good things will come to the talented if they merely desire it enough. Yet what is their success ultimately built on? A bedrock of deception and deceit.

Wall-E: Our fetishizing of technology becomes twisted as we begin to believe it must fetishize us in return, and will assist in rescuing us from our own self-destruction. Our mind is a hell we cannot escape from.

Up: Our life is a sad grasp for childhood dreams we made in the senseless blur of our youth, and either we will destroy them or be destroyed by them. What pitiful automatons we are in this cursed fable, never even a thought of what freedom may truly mean.

Toy Story 3: Here we see the true curse of consciousness, that it can conceive of its own end. Yet does this dithering fable see this through? No, it doesn't even look away, it covers it in a mass of lies. God is dead, yet some can do nothing more than conceive of new gods.

Cars 2: A pitiful play-act. We imagine a world where life is extinguished and machines carry forth the disease of consciousness, yet nothing more is imagined for them than recreations of

"Should we leave a note?"

our own dull fantasies of bravery and daring. We cannot even diagnose our illness properly.

Brave: What is its moral? That independence is a lie, that destiny is unforgiving, that family bonds are chains we pull at but cannot loosen. Flee from freedom, it brings only tragedy and undoing. The fairy tale of the complacent.

Monsters University: Ah, I see we could not truly imagine a world based on joy, so instead we retreat into the past. But do we face our revelation about the nature of fear in a capitalist society? No, we obscure it with comic hijinks, like a clown dancing before an abattoir.

Inside Out: The perfect corporate myth of human behavior, that the chaotic universe of the human psyche is so simple it is controlled by committee and true acceptance is achieved through reconciliation with the status quo. We blind ourselves to our true demons.

The Good Dinosaur: We can imagine a distant past and an alternate reality but not a radical new morality. Humans are envisioned as slavish animals and we indulge this dull fantasy of degradation because it amuses us, but does not threaten us.

Finding Dory: Memory is all we have that ties us to this world and we cling to it like shipwrecked sailors in a maelstrom grasping for whatever will float. Yet it is impermeable, and can pull us down forever. This film sees joy in it only

because it ignores the mad chaos.

Cars 3: When will the hell of consciousness end? We shall pass it along to each new generation and only total oblivion will spare us. We pretend the things we make are imbued with our sense of self, yet to imagine they will want more than we allow is beyond us. God cackles.

Coco: Even in death we do not escape our obligations to memory and to family. And death does not free us of them. Life is a prison, and this tale envisions that the only freedom from consciousness we have is to be forgotten. Obliteration is salvation, children. What horror.

The Incredibles 2: Another parable about the forces aligning against the true elites of the world as they try to wrestle power from them. It whispers that the concentration of power in elites' hands is good, because THEY are moral, unlike those others. This film is Satan.

Toy Story 4: A child creates a pitiful imitation of life and it screams in terror at the curse it has been given. The film whispers the lie that we are gods now, but the implication is that if God is real he put no more thought into us than a child would a half-made plaything.

—*Ryan Nyburg*

UH-OH.—*ED.*
I have just fashioned a uniquely brilliant cover letter that I plan to enclose with every submission in any and all media.

To wit:
"CAVEAT EMPTOR!

Upon acceptance, publication and (especially) even the tiniest remuneration to its creator, the attached manuscript/essay/painting/cartoon/drawing/design, the unrivaled and unbroken record of abysmal defeat and humiliation heretofore enjoyed by Laurie Frank Rosenwald, (*a.k.a.* Jolie-Laide Balloon), in a remarkably appalling career punctuated by heartbreak, disaster and misfortune, will be summarily annihilated. Rosenwald's unique reputation as a complete and utter failure in not one, but six respected professions is one of which the most degraded masochist can only dream.

It beggars belief that with unrelenting will and determination, in the face of contempt, scorn and ridicule this self-styled polymath consistently produces original…stuff, facing the kind of soul-crushing rejection that would obliterate any sane contender. Intrepid, she stubbornly persists, ceaselessly inflicting her insignificant "content" on a begrudging and disaffected audience. Each cataclysmic fiasco, invariably fated to implode on contact with the public, only seems to imbue her with fresh energy. Unfortunately.

Remember, should you choose to ignore this counsel and pursue the foolhardy endorsement of Miss Rosenwald's work, whether it be in the realm of graphic or product design, illustration, fine art, comedy or literature, any triumph could mean that a sustained history of unremitting, consecutive catastrophe would be instantly extinguished. If even one gallery exhibits her shamelessly derivative and unsightly paintings, if one publisher accepts one manuscript, a course of endless frustration will be derailed, and mediocrity allowed to flourish. We will not be held responsible. You have been forewarned.

Rosenwald's atrocious personality as a pitiable and neglected outsider is unbearable enough. Editors, art directors, publishers, producers and art dealers on five continents see eye to eye; she is a pain in the neck, nothing more. Australia and Antarctica have been mercifully spared Miss Rosenwald's tedious and pathetic solicitations.

Imagine, if you will, to what beastly, nefarious depths this delusional charlatan might sink, should worldly success touch her poisonous soul. Prosperity is out of the question. What arrogant, hideous monster would thus be created? The ego! How long must we suffer the unwelcome entreaties of this vituperative nag? People of Earth, should you choose to ignore this admonishment, let it be on your 7,745,059,168 heads.*

Take heed. Rosenwald shall not prevail!"

—Laurie Rosenwald

RE: THE POST-REVOLUTION TOPPLING OF OUR FORMER LEADER'S MASSIVE STATUE.

Last night, after a month-long Twitter campaign, our current regime crumbled and our Great Leader fled the country. Typically, this is when ebullient citizen groups celebrate by chanting slogans of renewal while toppling the statue of our former leader. But I say: let's not this time.

First, it's wasteful. That giant statue of our Great Leader took months to construct at a cost of over three million of our monetary units. The horse part was especially costly. At the time, we were all for it. We'd just been through a pretty tough coup, and the Great Leader was looking like he had the answers. Now that he's been disgraced, I understand the urge to attach some ropes to that sucker, hack it off at the base, and topple it dramatically for the camera crews. But then what? The next guy is just going to want another statue built of him—that's their thing—and we're the ones who'll have to foot the bill.

Given the state of our economy, can we really afford another three-million-monetary-unit project? Shouldn't we work on getting unspoiled meat back on the shelves before we invest in more giant statuary?

Here's my idea: Let's topple just the head. Less work, and almost as dramatic. We leave the body and the horse parts, and when the new leader comes to power, he only has to commission a new head for the top.

What if it's a woman, you say? Great joke!

I know some of you are already locating your hacksaws and rope in preparation, but I would counsel prudence. Toppling a perfectly salvageable statue not only doesn't make good fiscal sense, it also makes us look kind of fickle as a people. I mean, weren't we hacksawing down a slightly smaller statue of our previous leader only a decade ago?

Also, think about this: despots sometimes return from exile and rise to prominence again with a new, whitewashed past. Who do you think our returning Great Leader will pick first for the firing squads? After the previous leader, that is. I'll tell you who: those who demolished his pet project, the topplers of the massive and exorbitantly expensive statue in his honor.

So let's take just the head. I think it could be a real crowd-pleaser. We can lower it down with our ropes, cheer victoriously—all the usual stuff—then wrap it up carefully for storage, just in case.

Vive la Révolution!

—K. A. Polzin

* Calculated as of this afternoon.

FAKE NEWS, 1948.

(The following Corrections section appeared in *The Chicago Daily Tribune*, November 4th, 1948.)

Masthead, page 1: The headline from yesterday's *Tribune*, "DEWEY DEFEATS TRUMAN" was inaccurate. It was based on early, partial returns, but—we will admit it!— was *also* influenced by our nigh-irresistible urge to see Thomas Dewey's mustachioed lip curling into that wonderful, boyish smile all Republicans have grown to treasure. In retrospect, we should have waited for *all* the results to come in, rather than printing what we *fervently believed* would be the choice of a hitherto-sane American populace, clearly driven utterly insensate by sybaritic Socialism.

Also, it must be said that our Typesetting Department urged us to go to press as early as possible, so we could immediately begin composing subsequent front pages reflecting "the outpouring of worldwide adulation that would herald the new Golden Age of Tom."

We now realize that was a joke or something.

While our desire to be the first to publicly coronate a public servant as

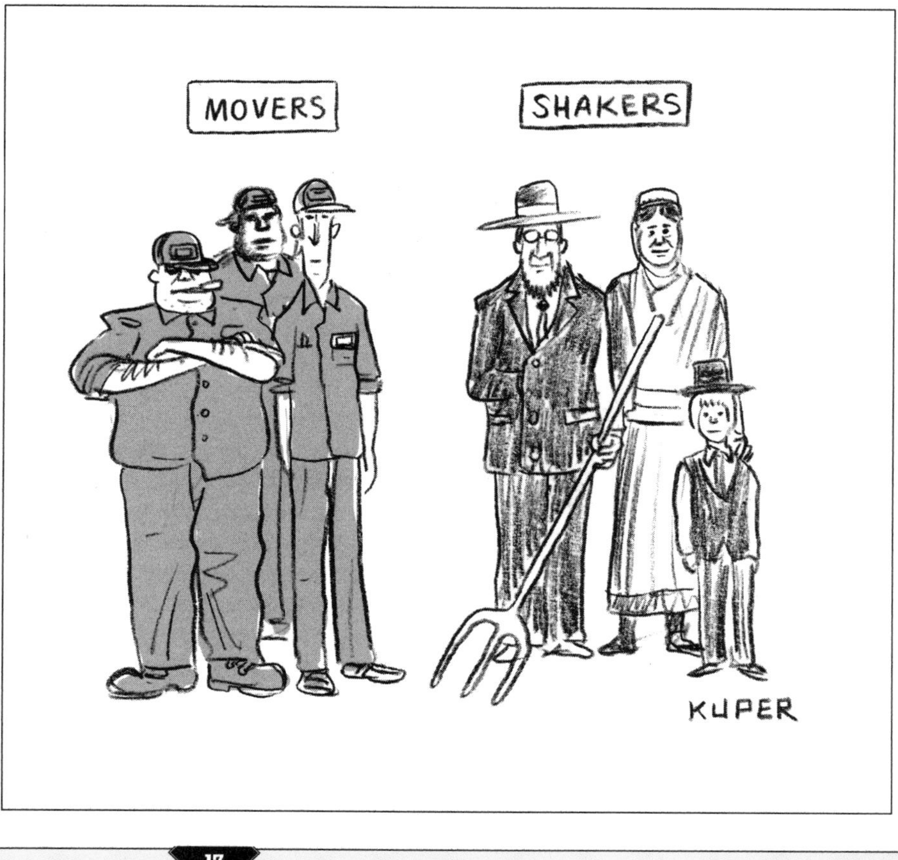
MOVERS
SHAKERS
KUPER

"Help! It's got my phone!"

intelligent, principled, and roguishly handsome as Thomas Dewey is something we will *never* apologize for, we do sincerely regret spreading misinformation, causing hurt or embarrassment to the Dewey family, and providing photo ops for a certain braying Missouri jackass.

Style, page 12: "Facial Hair: The Next Big Look in Presidential Grooming," appears now to also be flawed. While we stand by "the dashing lip-fur of President-elect Dewey," we acknowledge that, incredibly, tragically, he is not the Chief Executive to-be.

Additionally, our declaration that "every future occupant of the White House will have a full beard, luscious mustache, or at the very least thick, robust muttonchops" appears to be yet another good thing ruined by that son of a bitch T****n.

About Town, page 18: "Jubilant Dewey supporters should come out to Lincoln Park early today, as crowds will be large and happy, brass bands will be playing, and the lines for cider will be long, as the temperature is predicted to reach a balmy 65 degrees."*

---
*This rumor appears to have originated in our Typesetting Department.

As you likely know, the dozens of Dewey revelers who came out were whipped by icy winds, and soaked to the bone by a torrent of freezing rain that, at the time of this writing, continues unabated. Additionally, there was no cider.

Obituary, page 34: "Annie Louise Dewey, mother of Governor Thomas Dewey, has died in a whorehouse fire." This is not correct; our lawyers tell us that Mrs. Dewey is alive and well and apparently filing a lawsuit. We would like to apologize to her, and the rest of the Dewey family, who we are amazed made it that far into yesterday's edition.

As is common, the *Tribune*'s Obituary section keeps brief biographies of the family members of all Presidential nominees; yesterday's edition had been widely distributed before the relevant editors realized that this one particular obit had been written, apparently in jest, by a now-fired typesetter who is a T***** supporter and a Communist... but we repeat ourselves.

The Tribune sincerely regrets the errors.—*Col. Robert R. McCormick, Publisher.*

—*Ritch Duncan*

IDEAS FOR HOW TO GET MORE PEOPLE TO COME TO MY NEW GROCERY STORE.

- Ask people very nicely to please come to the store.
- Hide a "golden lime" somewhere in the store—the first to find it gets to take the lime home and keep it for three days, after which time they must hide it somewhere else in the store for the next person to find.
- Get rid of the wolves.
- Put out a large sign saying, "Free Nudie Pictures Here," and hope that once they walk in, they'll be so impressed with the store that they won't even notice that all the pictures are of apricots, and all the apricots are dressed in sensible pantsuits.
- Stop dressing all the produce in sensible pantsuits.
- Go door-to-door with a picture of a different, worse grocery store, showing it to people and telling them that my grocery store is much better than that one.
- Get the grocery store listed as one of *TIME Magazine*'s 100 Most Influential People.
- Consider installing a door of some kind.

—*Adam Chase*

LUFT: SCANDINAVIA'S PREMIER AIRSHIP RIDE-SHARING APP.

[The Bystander *would like to thank Google Translate for the translation from Swedish.—Ed.*]

Has this happened to you: extended toil at the business office, exerting within the machinery of modern endeavor, effort upon effort toward the important presentation? You exit the structure depleted of vigor, longing for the leisure of home. You engage your preferred ride-sharing app; once inside the Toyota Camry, and while observing the suggestive stain upon the seat, the fragrant driver announces a fact of unpleasantness: congestion occurs on the expeditious route. Arrival at your domicile is delayed hours.

What if you could just float above the turmoil? That's the concept of Luft.

Initially developed for traversing the archipelagos and fjords of Scandinavia, Luft, the world's first app-based dirigible ridesharing platform, is now engaging riders across the United States. It works in the following way: When circumstances require you to rise above the machinations of progress, simply engage the Luft app and program your destination. Then, a local airship enthusiast will plot a course to your location (or nearby mooring mast). Once your transport has arrived, you will simply undergo a brief frisk to exclude any sharp objects or incendiary devices.

Now feel the unencumbered majesty of airship travel! You and your destination could be reunited in as little as three hours, all without the eternal anguish and dense constipation of automobile travel.

Name the thing that you are waiting for! Our fleet of hot air balloons is ready to engage riders! We are dedicated to efficiently moving your body (and one personal item) from its current location to a new location selected by you!

I know your thoughts: "What if my desires include the premium airship experience?" It is unnecessary to speak further: Introducing Luft Stratos. Luft Stratos offers the unique experience of airship travel for riders marinating in the sumptuous lifestyle. (A reminder: with the choice of Luft Stratos, many hours of preparation may be required to prepare your zeppelin, semi-rigid dirigible, or blimp. Additionally, we often declaim to Luft Stratos riders that containing a snack may have a preferable outcome.)

One feedback of frequency is: I am with passion for the Luft experience, but when I measure my daily regimen against the elapsing of time, there is a shortcoming. This is feedback that we have noted vigorously! For this reason we have implemented Luft Pronto.

Luft Pronto utilizes Skyhook technology developed by U.S. Government Central Intelligence Agency as a way to offer expedited egress. Simply allow the helium balloon to draw the 150 meter steel cable into the air, adorn yourself with the attached safety harness, and sit with your back facing the wind. One of our amateur airplane enthusiasts will fly overhead and seize the balloon from the bosom of the sky, whisking you away from your current location while hoisting your body (and one personal item) into the cargo bay of the airplane. Once inside, riders can attach themselves to the provided parachute and simply debark from the airplane when appropriate, drifting down toward the vicinity of their business meeting, social engagement, or urgent hospital stay.

When you just need to get somewhere without the mental discomfort and frustration of automobiles interlocked in the coitus of rush hour, or if you just desire to float, Luft is available for your enjoyment and carriage!

—Maxx Ziegler

REAL ESTATE.

All right team, we're aiming to build the most terrifying house possible. So here's the game plan:

First things first, we're in Victorian-era England, where most of the houses look haunted already. So, good job, we have that going for us.

In terms of the exterior, we need to fill the backyard area with a ton of creepy-ass vegetation. My suggestion would be the Great Banyan Tree, *Ficus benghalensis*, native to India. The trunk looks like it's made of several strands of tree hairs, and the branches naturally spread out in an eerie spider-like fashion, which is the general vibe that we're going for.

Next, the foundation. What we're really looking for is a foundation that is simultaneously massive and flimsy. Ideally, it would be cool if on windy days, the house could kind of sway back and forth like an interpretive dancer. Creaking is key. Where is it coming from? *Everywhere*.

We need to decide at some point if we're using wood or bricks. If we use wood, we gotta make sure it's the kind that looks like it's been semi-terrorized by termites. If we use bricks, we gotta get the crumbly kind. (Which, bonus, will be cheap.)

The shape of this house is really important because it frames the interior. Make it pointy on the tops, very pointy, and long and scary for the main parts.

Now let's talk interior.

People often poetically quote that the

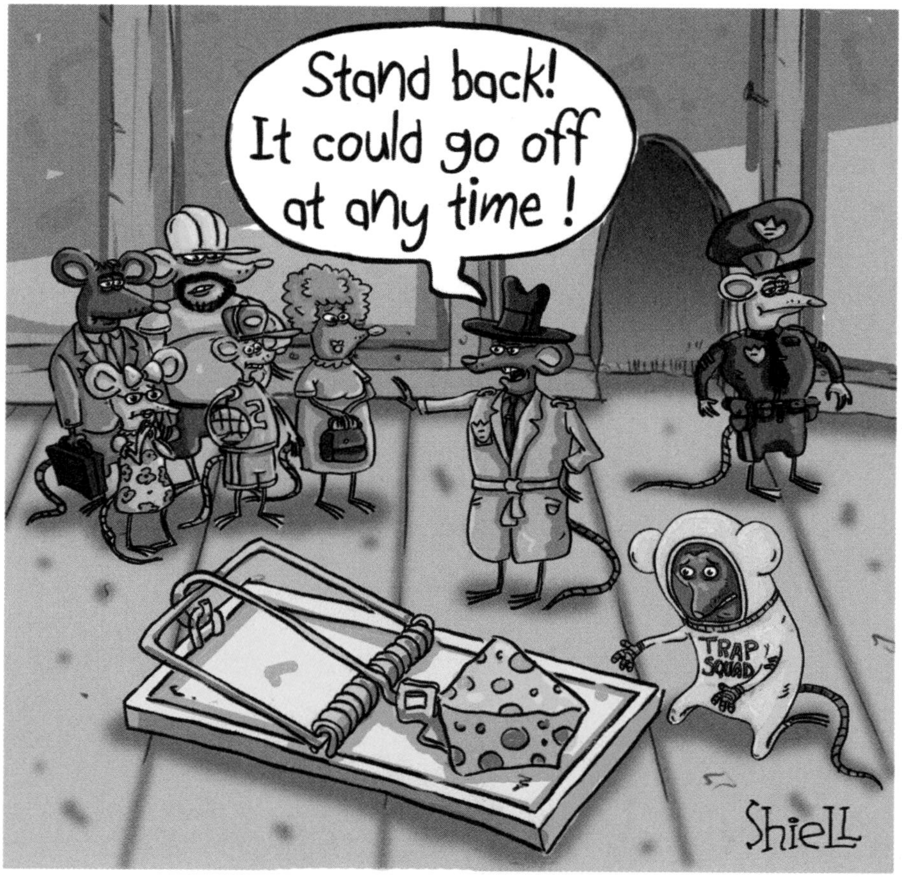
Stand back! It could go off at any time!
TRAP SQUAD
ShieLL

eyes are the windows to the soul. Riffing off of that, we want to make our windows the rotting teeth of this house. I want them stained. I want them smelling weird all the time. I want them shrouded by a large, preferably red, curtain. And I know this is ambitious, but it would be optimal if we could get someone, maybe once a month, to stand in the window at night. Just…looking.

And then when a passerby, like a kid on a bike, takes notice, they would quickly pull the curtains closed as if to imply to that passerby, "We got secrets and some *nefarious shit* is happening up in here."

We have two options for the overall look of the interior: completely empty or completely furnished. If empty, we want white sheets over all the furniture and a cloudy sheen over all the mirrors, as if they have cataracts. If completely furnished, we want full Versailles décor, gold emblems, huge oil paintings of some dead kings and stuff, a grand piano, the works.

Regardless of which route we take, there will be a locked door near the basement *no matter what.*

Okay. Now we want to add a finishing touch to elevate this house from "terrifying" to "unholy." We get a murder of crows to circle the top of the house—

like the chimney area, and maybe the turret—on every cloudy day. Yes, we'll have to train them. And there's no better guy for the job than Tommy, our crow guy. Call Tommy. Yeah, call Tommy now.

Finally, we place this house in the center of this dump called "London." In two hundred years, this sucker'll be worth a cool ten million dollars.

—*Jennifer Kim*

PINOCCHIO RUNS FOR OFFICE.

Folks, don't be fooled by all the
   phony buzz:
I'm no one's puppet, and I never was.
I didn't torture an endangered whale.
At Pleasure Island, I did not inhale.

You say you've seen the footage? It's
   all wonky—
I'm solid GOP, no hint of donkey.
My only kind of "circus"? Media.
(Ignore those pics on Wikipedia.)

And what about the rumor—so damn
   nasty!—
that constant lying led to rhinoplasty
at some chic clinic north of Bimini?
A smear by my opponent, Jiminy.

—*Melissa Balmain* B

CERISE ZELENETZ

"BOYLAN'S WRY WIT, WICKED SENSE OF HUMOR, AND UNIQUE WAY OF TURNING PHRASES SHINE THROUGH…"

~KIRKUS REVIEWS

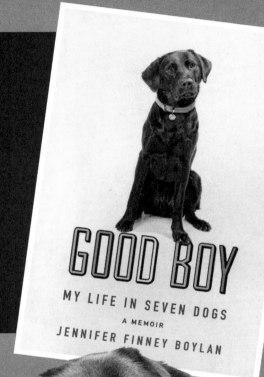

GOOD BOY

MY LIFE IN SEVEN DOGS

A NEW MEMOIR BY JENNIFER FINNEY BOYLAN, *NEW YORK TIMES* BESTSELLING AUTHOR OF *SHE'S NOT THERE: A LIFE IN TWO GENDERS*

"*Good Boy* is a warm, funny, instantly engaging testament to the power of love—canine and human—to ease us through life's radical transitions. And I say that as a cat person!"

~JENNIFER EGAN
Winner of the Pulitzer Prize and author of *A Visit from the Goon Squad* and *Manhattan Beach*

"Dogs help us understand ourselves: who we are, who we've been. They teach us what it means to love, and to be loved. They bear witness to our joys and sorrows; they lick the tears from our faces. And when our backs are turned, they steal a whole roasted chicken off the supper table."

~JENNIFER FINNEY BOYLAN

ON SALE
APRIL 21, 2020
PRE-ORDER NOW

CELADONBOOKS.COM/BOOKSHOP

BY JACK HANDEY

TOOTHPICK

Much pickin', but no grinnin'

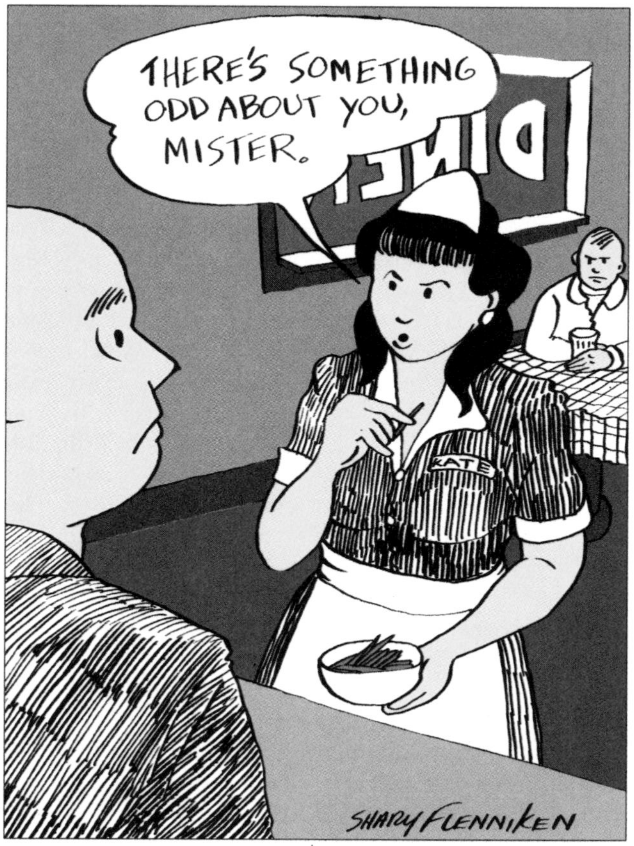
THERE'S SOMETHING ODD ABOUT YOU, MISTER.
KATE
DINER
SHARY FLENNIKEN

On March 17, 1993, Ted Manion was at a reception at the White House. While chatting with President Clinton, he happened to have a toothpick in his mouth. When the President came to the punch line of a joke he was telling, Manion laughed so hard the toothpick flew out of his mouth and stuck in the President's face. Chased from the room by Secret Service agents, Manion became a fugitive.

A few months later he found himself seated at a diner in the desert Southwest.

"How was the pie?" said the waitress.

"Fine. It was fine," said Manion.

"You're not from around here, are you?" said the waitress.

"No, just passing through. If I could get my check..."

"How about a toothpick?" she said.

"Uh, no thanks," said Manion.

"Come on," said the waitress. "I make them myself. I carve 'em and I paint 'em different colors and everything."

Manion grew nervous. "No, really, I'd rather not."

Another customer, seated at the counter, chimed in. "You should try one, stranger. She dips 'em in cinnamon oil. They taste great."

Manion was firm but polite. "Look, I don't want a toothpick. I just want my check."

The waitress eyed him suspiciously. "There's something odd about you, mister."

Another patron approached. "Yeah, I've been watching you. You seem awful nervous about something."

"Okay, okay," said Manion, "I'll have a toothpick."

The waitress offered him a bowl of toothpicks. Manion took one and stuck it in his mouth. The two other customers seemed to relax.

A sheriff 's car pulled up out front, and a deputy entered with a big rolled-up poster under his arm.

"Hi, Kate," said the deputy.

"Hi, Carl. Whatcha got there?"

"Just got in a new 'Wanted' poster. Mind if I put it up right here, behind the counter?"

The deputy taped up the poster. It was Manion! In shock, he spit out the toothpick. The waitress screamed. The toothpick was embedded in her cheek.

Five years later, Manion was executed in the electric chair. As the surge of electricity hit him, he spit out the toothpick that was in his mouth from his last meal. The toothpick stuck in the eye of the warden. **B**

JACK HANDEY *is best known for his "Deep Thoughts." He's a contributor to* **The New Yorker** *and other publications. His latest book,* **Please Stop the Deep Thoughts**, *can be ordered on JackHandey.com.*

BY LOU BEACH

TOURISM

How Spewing Death Mountain came to be

THERE IS a volcano nearby. It sits at the edge of the forest like a giant anthill. It is mostly dormant but occasionally emits a half-hearted puff of smoke and a sad dribble of lava just to remind us who's who around here, though it hasn't erupted and caused any damage since my grandmother's time.

One year the elders decided to encourage tourism and bought an ad the size of a child's finger in the back of *The New Yorker*, a magazine they were assured was read by only the wealthiest Americans. The assurer was a villager who had gone to New York City in the spring to seek his fortune but returned shortly thereafter with only a clock radio and a broken heart.

Several new huts were erected at the outskirts of the village to accommodate the anticipated visitors, decorated and furnished in the latest bamboo style. A fire pit was dug nearby and a shiny new cooking pot was hung over it. A souvenir stand was set up at the base of the volcano to sell T-shirts. The shirts were emblazoned with a picture of the volcano spewing flowers instead of lava, and the word WELCOME in yellow letters.

Months went by before the bus finally dropped off a group of visitors. A nun had brought four blind orphans, hoping the volcano might somehow provide a miraculous restoration of their sight. They were housed in the new huts and a celebratory meal was prepared in the new pot and we all sat around and watched the blind children eat with their hands.

The next morning we set off for the volcano with the nun and children, my friends and I acting as guides. When we arrived, the nun dispensed silver coins to us with instructions to climb up and throw the coins into the volcano's smoky mouth, to hasten the miracle. She and the children stayed below to pray. We picked our way up carefully and when we'd gotten to the top and stood looking into the smelly hole, some of my friends only pretended to throw their coins in, tucking them instead into their cheeks, but I was afraid of bad luck and sin, and tossed mine with a flourish, my eyes shut tight, a prayer in my heart.

The blind children did not recover their sight, but they returned to the new huts and remained in the village along with the nun, who eventually discarded her nun getup and dressed like a villager and married a handsome headman. They are all a part of us now.

No more tourists came and the bus eventually stopped running. The souvenir stand blew over in a storm and the T-shirts were doled out to my friends and me. The boys wore them with pride and thought we should form a gang called The Lava Lords, but the girls said that was stupid and didn't want to be in a gang so we all decided to form a rock band instead. We called ourselves Spewing Death Mountain and sat around the fire pit every night beating on the big pot while the ex-nun and the blind children danced. B

LOU BEACH *is an artist, writer, and award-winning illustrator living in Los Angeles.*

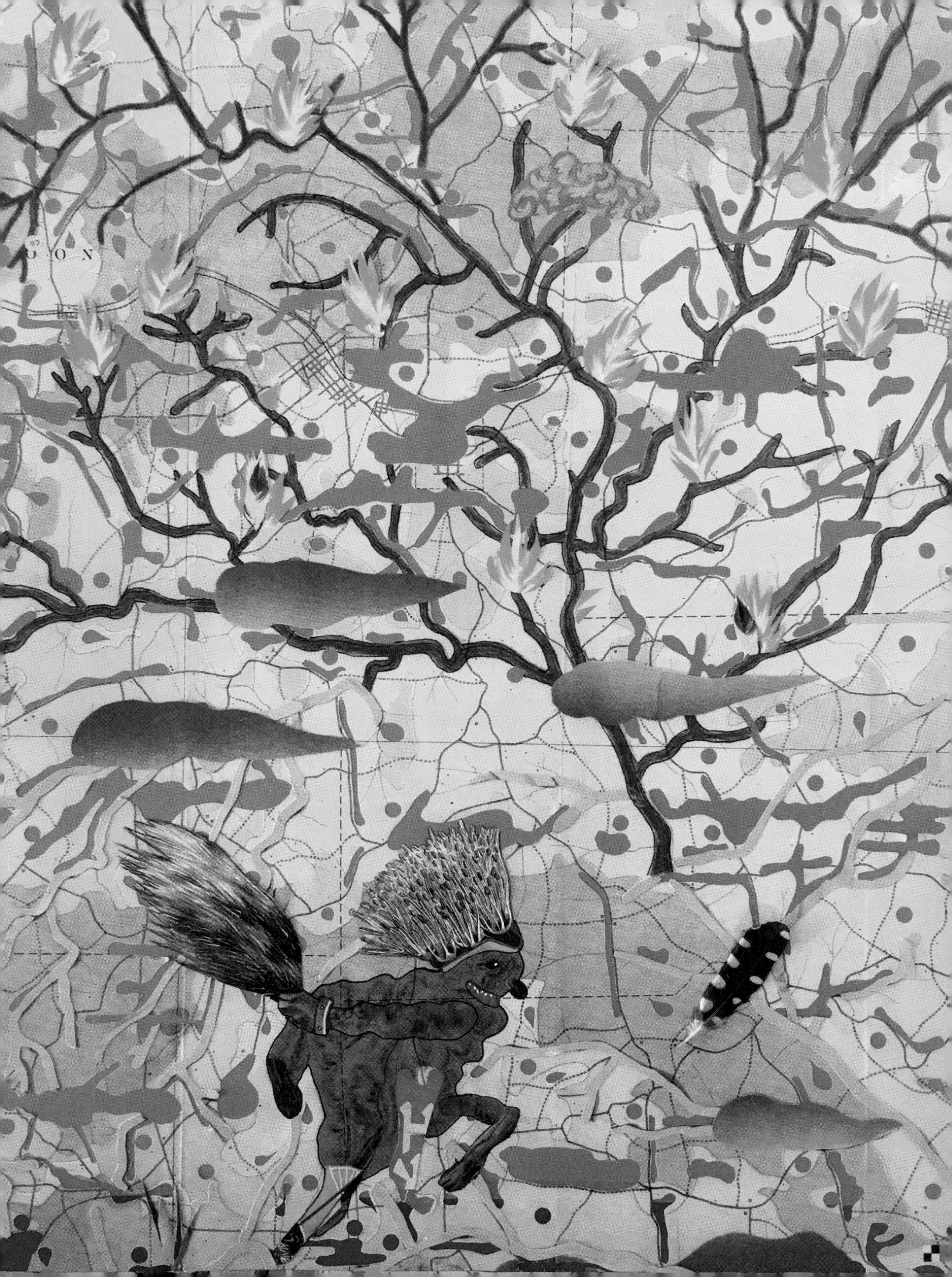

BY JENN KNOTT

ASK JABBA

Let an enormous, extraterrestrial slug gangster solve your relationship problems

Dear Jabba,
Have you ever lived in the suburbs? I hope not, because they suck *ass*. Problem is, my husband commutes to work and loves living here, somehow missing the fact that I'm dying here. Jabba, I *have* to live in a city. Even murder-y, drug-infested Detroit! How can I convince Hubs to relocate? I'm desperate enough to withhold sex.
Wasting Away in West Bloomfield

Dear Sad Indentured House Servant,
Strengthen yourself! Only frigid Hoth is truly uninhabitable. "De-troit" sounds utterly delightful.

As a hermaphrodite, I cannot relate to anything having to do with sexual intercourse, which I find absurdly complex and utterly repellent. But as your counselor, I can tell you this: differences in opinion cannot be changed, only punished.
Activate trap door to
the Rancor pit,
Jabba the Hutt

Dear Mr. Hutt,
Check out my wife's new "healthy" diet plan: no dairy, no wheat, and *no meat*. I'm a man, Mr. Hutt. Men need protein.

It's been going on for two weeks now. Last night, she tried to pass off a steaming pile of colly-flower mash and Zachariah ribbons as "pizza." How do I get my old food back?
Starving & Sick Of It

Dear Sick Man,
I too endure great misery when an hour passes without live flesh sliding down my capacious gullet.

Send your most disposable slaves into the sewers to hunt for amphibious Gorgs. When they return, savor the still-twitching animals while you enjoy the entertainment of the Rancor disemboweling the servant who brought the least bounty.
Koonyah mahlyass koong,
Jabba

Dear Jabba Desilijic Tiure,
After the birth of our twins, my husband has stopped wanting sex. I'm lonely, and my feelings are hurt; I work out and still look *damn good* for somebody whose body was a two-passenger submarine this time last year. How do I get him more interested in me than in Netflix? I'm willing to try new locations, weird positions, whatever.
Hot & Bothered Mama

Dear Woman Doing Something Wrong,
How many girl slaves and dancers do you keep in your villa? If you and your mate are traffickers of any importance, my guess is around six.

Does your husband dress them in brassieres of pure copper and loincloths of crimson silk? Does he reel them in on their chain-leashes, demanding they caress his endless rubbery folds? Does he kiss them with lips dripping in putrid slime and flick at them with his giant, muscular tongue?

If not, he might be gay.
His Excellency J. the H.

Dear Moron,
This is a warning to all readers out there. My wife and I took your advice and—guess what, Jabba? *We're both going to jail!*

You're not a licensed therapist. You're not married. You're not even human. Just because you're the Outer Rim's most influential and dangerous crime worm, you think you know everything. But all your so-called "helpful hints" are the psychopathic fantasies of an orally fixated sadist.

Like idiots, we wrote you. Like idiots, we stole that newborn. Now, like idiots, we're f*cked.
Seeing Through the Fraud

Dear You're the Moron,
Who seeks to topple the great intergalactically syndicated Jabba Desilijic Tiure of Nal Hutta with petty insults and speciesist slurs?

Would you were in my palace on Tatooine, I would order my captive underground beast to snap off your limbs like the brittle twigs from a withered Tuanulberry bush! Then I would chortle happily as your worthless blood poured over the ancient stones of my inescapable dungeon.

As you are not in my palace, I suggest you offer yourself to the nearest wampa. *If* it will have you.
Chool kanya wee shaja mee-choo,
Jabba the Hutt, Infallible

Dear Lord Jabba,
I'm desperate for a temporary escape from my whole family! Any hot tips for a relaxing weekend getaway?
Mommy Needs a Recharge

Dear Quitter Mom,
I've heard nice things about De-troit, presumably in your star system? B

JENN KNOTT (@jkusesherwords) is a comedy writer in Bavaria, Germany. She dearly hopes for a Ghost of Jabba cameo in the final Star Wars movie, and that you check her out at jennknott.com.

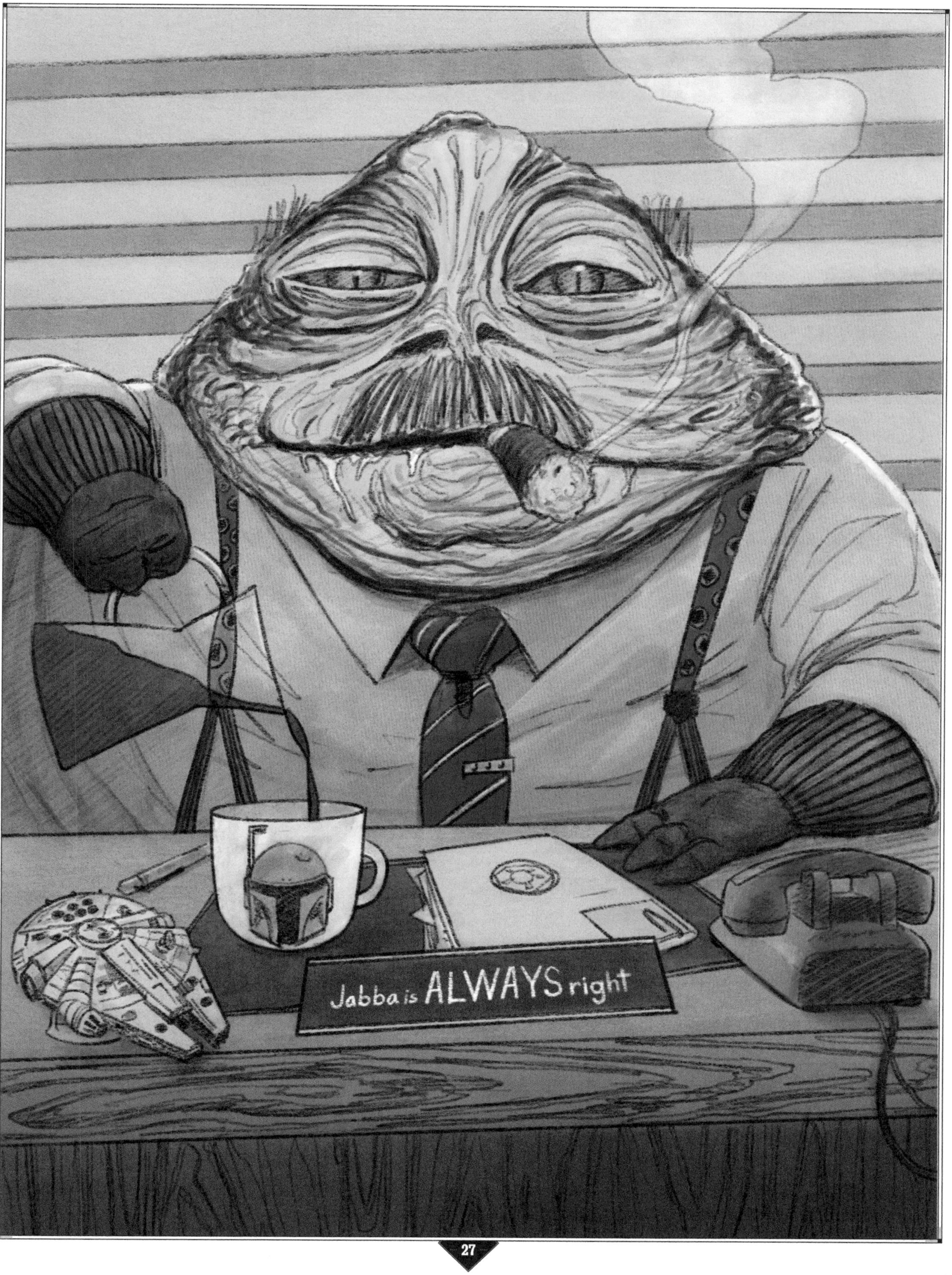
Jabba is ALWAYS right

BY BEN DOYLE

A COWBOYLAND MANIFESTO

Remember: holsters are NOT for cell phones

1: WE WILL EMBRACE OUR INNER COWBOY

We will first and foremost embrace our Cowboy name, which is "Cowboy + [our given name]," unless our given name is unconvincing, in which case our Cowboy name is "Cowboy Earl." We will wear a big hat and grow a moustache. If we cannot grow a moustache, we will purchase an authentic "Rootin' Tootin' Cowboy 'Stache" at the PleasurePark gift shop. We will not break from our Cowboy persona for any reason. We will not give our personal phone number to guests of PleasurePark. If a guest offers their phone number to us, we will say "Dadgummit, Missy, what in tarnation is a *tel-e-phone*?" We will say this even if the guest is very beautiful.

We will only eat Cowboy food during work hours, which is limited to the following:

- Tinned beans;
- tinned hominy;
- hardtack (tinned or untinned);
- salt pork;
- chewing "tobacky"; and
- anything available for purchase at Ho-Down Harry's Authentic Nacho Stand

(*Please* note: As per the recent SCOTUS decision, *China National Entertainment Corporation v. Tumbleweed Sam*, neither CNEC, nor it subsidiaries, holdings, or principals, regardless of region or jurisdiction, have any liability for health problems caused by the above diet.)

2: WE WILL NOT POINT OUR SIX-SHOOTERS AT THE GUESTS

This should go without saying, but in light of recent events it must be repeated that guests are not to be "robbed," "hornswoggled," or "forced to dance at gunpoint." We accept that this may be inauthentic, especially when guests are obvious greenhorns and wearing "purty" jewelry. If we feel that it's *absolutely necessary* to rob a guest, we will announce it loudly and in front of witnesses, *e.g.*, "Why you Eastern city slicker, I oughta rob you good!" and then

we will chase them, but slowly, modulating our speed even further in the case of the elderly or a child. If they fall down, we will pretend to lose track of where they went, while surreptitiously pressing the Medi-Alert buckle on our Cowboy Belt. If a guest pulls a gun on us, we will "skedaddle" (*e.g.*, hide behind a rain barrel). *We will never return fire at a guest.* We will only point our six-shooters at Biggie Bear, designated jugs, shootin' cans, animatronic varmints, and on Sundays, Tumbleweed Sam.

3: WE WILL NOT "VAPE" IN FRONT OF THE GUESTS

If we must vape, we will vape in the Cast Member Recreation Shed before 6 am or after 11 pm. We will never vape in costume. We will not hide a Juul under our hat, because another Cowboy might shoot our hat off for fun and expose it. Instead of vaping, we will chaw, using branded spit-cups whenever not doing so would cause damage to CowboyLand or any other CNEC property. If we must smoke for medical reasons, we will limit ourselves to between six and twenty-four hand-rolled cigarettes a day, which we will roll in the recreation shed during "midday vittles." We will *not* hide marijuana in our cigarettes. If we have cigarettes left over at the end of the day, we will bring them to Sheriff Zhang, so that they may be easily deducted from our paychecks.

4: WE WILL NOT LEAVE COWBOYLAND FOR ANY REASON

Unless we are reassigned to Little Appalachia, SpacePlace, Giuseppe's Sicilian Adventure, or another PleasurePark district, we will not leave CowboyLand. We will not visit Daisy's Itty Bitty Petting Farm and begin "wrangling" the baby animals. We will not point our six-shooters at Daisy. We will not flirt with Daisy. We will not cook Daisy's baby animals over the spit in Russler's Corral for "midday vittles," no matter how authentic this would be. Even if it is very

BEN DOYLE (*@thewheatgerm*) is one of the finest comedy writers currently working in Providence, the "New York City" of Northern Rhode Island.

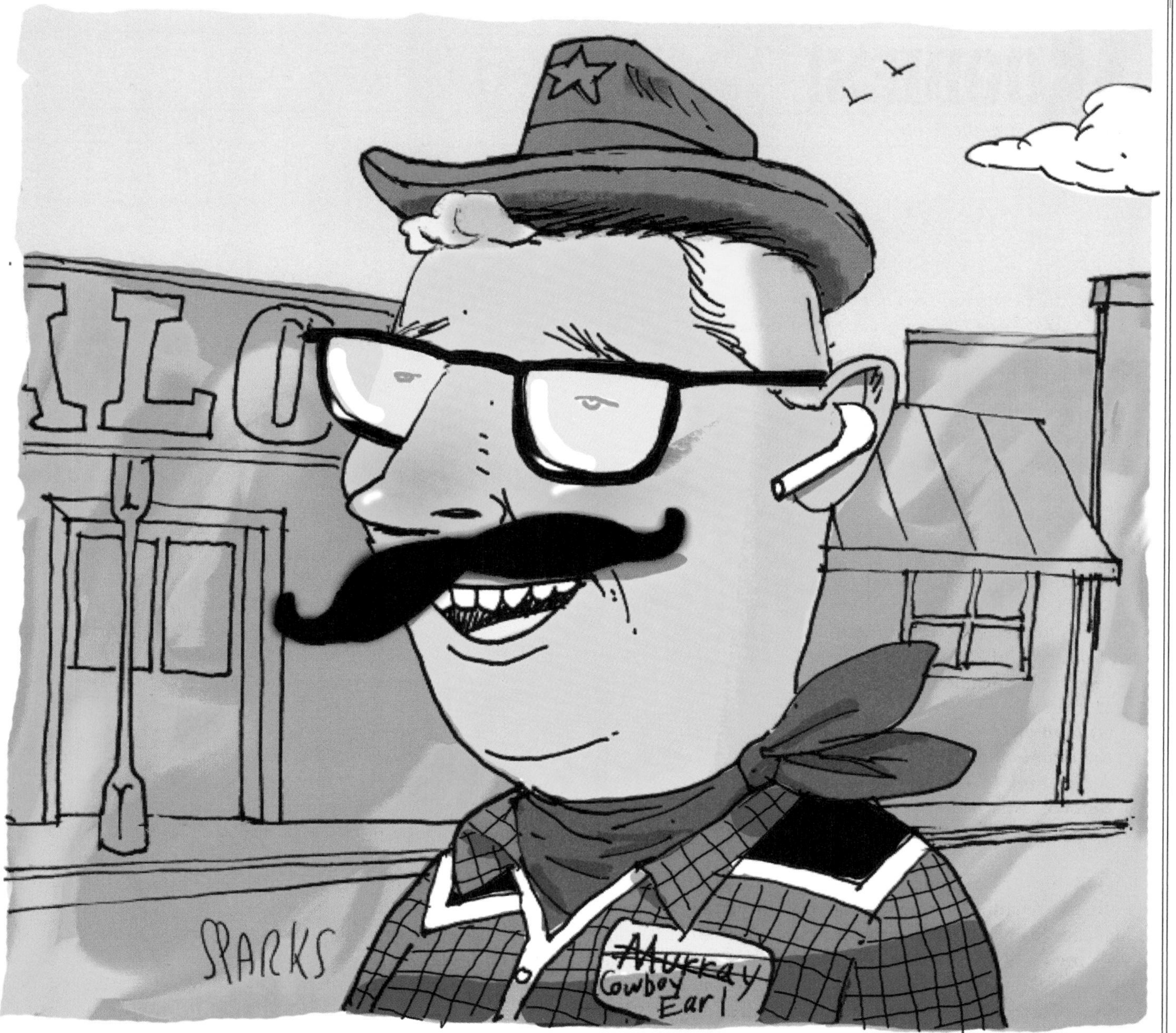
SPARKS
Murray
Cowboy Earl

hot out and CowboyLand is very dry from the dust-blowing machines, we will not disguise ourselves as guests and visit WetWorld. If CowboyLand is on fire, we will fight it in character until the Fire Department arrives, *with the lawyers*, at which point we will exit the park through PleasurePark's state-of-the-art sewer tunnels. If the sewer tunnels are on fire, we will accept our fates with Cowboy dignity, as per "Cowboy Jean-Paul's Rules of Conduct in an Uncaring Universe," posted 24/7 in the Cast Member Recreation Shed.

5: WE WILL NOT UNIONIZE, AND IF WE DO NOT KNOW WHAT THAT MEANS, WE WILL NOT GOOGLE IT

We will not ask Sheriff Zhang what a union is because, as stated many times, the Sheriff "don't cotton to such foolishness." If we continue to "pester him clear to tarnation," we accept that Sheriff Zhang, and/or the appropriate CNEC executives, may be forced to call in the Pinkertons to "whop us *good*." We will not read any pamphlets handed to us. If we are unhappy with the insurance situation, we will remember that real Cowboys had neither vision nor dental, and yet never once complained about "chronic gingivitis." We will not speak to a member of the press about our chronic gingivitis. If a member of the press requests a copy of this manifesto, we will turn around and pretend like we didn't hear them. If they say, "I know you can hear me, please, I want to help you," we will go get Sheriff Zhang, who will deal with it. We will not read this manifesto out loud, and if we already did, we will laugh now, and pretend like it was all one big joke. B

BY LAURIE ROSENWALD, 38C

BOOBIES!

Meet the twins

Rain forests were denuded of rare ebonies, mahoganies and teaks, Carrara's rockiest coastline blasted to powdery smithereens for exquisite Statuario marbles, to forge, in my father's sculpture studio, every imaginable iteration of the female form, all featuring proud, spherical... breasts. Bob Rosenwald's work was like Henry Moore's, only *bustier.*

All sculptors have their own interpretation of the *tata.* And of course, there's one question we've gotta nip in the bud: Nipples? Yes or no?

It depends who you ask.

Bernini: "Si!"

Rodin: "Ça depend!"

Michelangelo: "Assolutamente!"

Calder: "Huh?"

Picasso: "Raramente."

Moore: "Never."

Giacometti: "Stai scherzando?"

Brâncuși: "Nu!"

Jeff Koons: "Yes, but only on poodles."

Botero: "And how!"

Praxiteles: Εξαρτάται "από την αρχαία.

Call 'em tits, bazooms, gazongas, tig ole' bitties, milk helmets, fleshmelons, meat balloons, funbags, knockers, jugs, bee stings, hooters, sweater puppies or shirt turnips, Bob, my daddy-o, modeled them in plasticine, picrite, and Play-doh. He lost them in wax and found them again in bronze. He carved them out of alabaster, basalt, limestone, sandstone, soapstone and silly putty! Yes, lignum vitae is an endangered wood, but—so what? We're talkin' boobies here!

My mother, Ruth, a zaftig 38D, was his muse. Arms or legs would have only distracted from the main events of his masterpiece, a torso of her bodacious bod in oak. Let's just say she was stacked.

A more intimate collaboration between the gifted sculptor and my shapely mother resulted in their ultimate creation: my bad self. By the time I came along, Bob had mastered the art of the boob. Trust me on this.

My breasts are perfectly matched. They're not too pointy, they're not too globe-y. They're not too big. They're not too small. They are extra-medium!

They have personality, and here and there, just for fun, a strategically-placed mole. They are natural, organic, and may contain antioxidants. After all, nobody has said that they don't.

My breasts are sexy. My breasts are popular. Ask around. My breasts are lucrative! Okay, I did lease the left one to one Bruce W. in 1970. But the right one is still up for grabs. As it were.

My breasts are magnetic, like a built-in compass! Their sense of direction is infallible. Wherever I go, there they are. Where would I be without them? Possibly Jersey City.

My breasts are inspirational. Do you know that song, "Just the Two of Us"? It could have been written for my breasts. It wasn't, but it could have been.

The effect my breasts have had on men has been immeasurable. What I mean by this is that it has never been measured. Passionate painters, princes and poets, pirates, paramedics, pretzel-twisters, philologists and comparative literature students: all have found illumination in my voluptuositudinousness. And why not? When I put on my Black Satin Agent Provocateur Seraphina Plunge Balconette, watch out: Cleavage-R-Us. My breasts crave attention. And baby, they get what they want.

Although they can be quite a handful, they have a good attitude, I think. They're fun to be with, that's the word on the street. So even when you're down in the dumps, get cheered up by my lovely ladylumps!

My breasts are native New Yorkers, and of this they are justifiably (if somewhat irrationally) proud.

All in all, my breasts are outstanding! By the way, why are farmers like Nobel prize winners? Because they're outstanding in their fields. My breasts love a good clean joke. Why did the mushroom go to the party? Because he's a fungi!

And why did my breasts go to the party? *Stai scherzando?* Because *I* did, Bernini! 🅱

LAURIE ROSENWALD *(@rosenworld) is a painter, designer and author of* All The Wrong People Have Self-Esteem. *You can find her at www.rosenworld.com.*

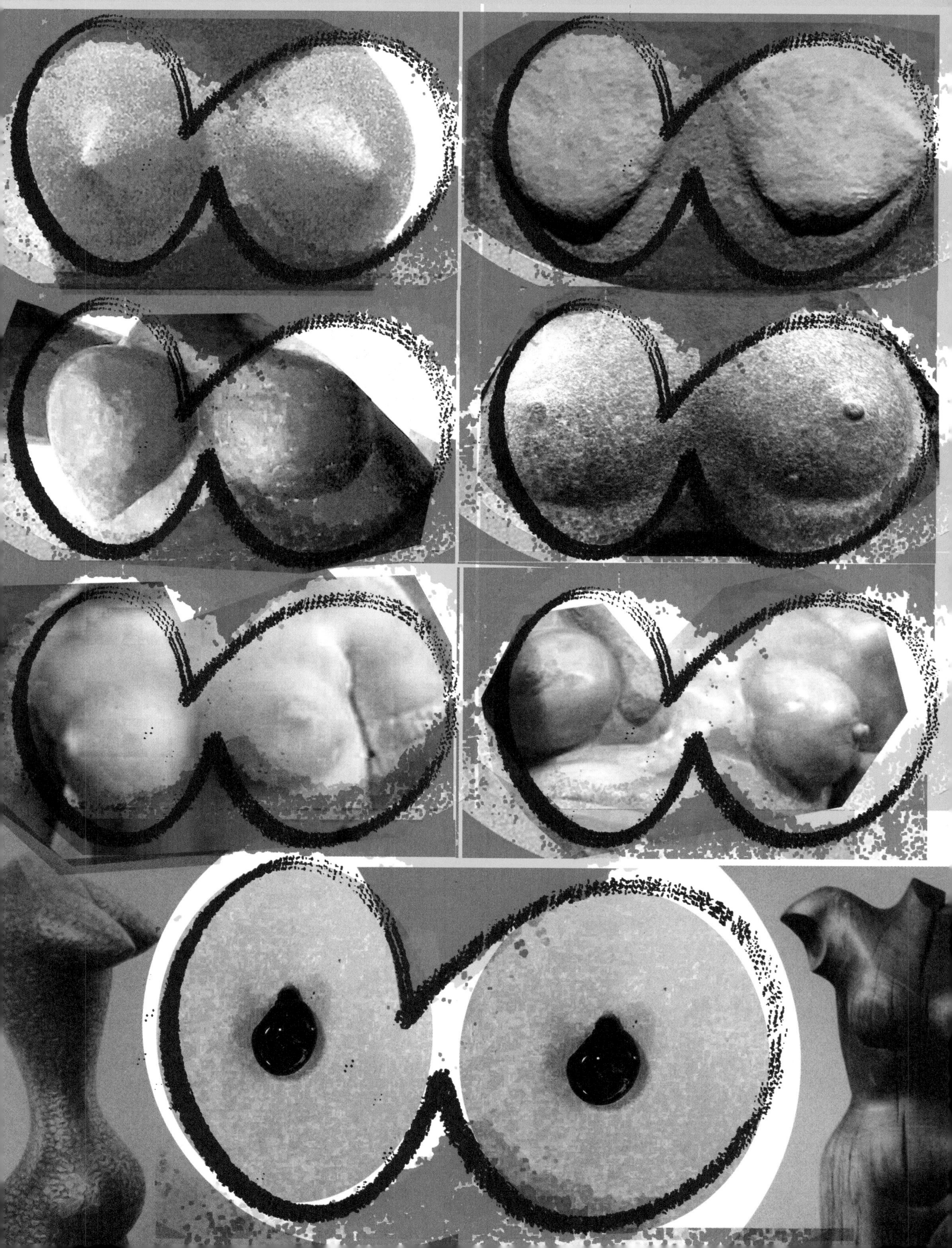

BY MEG FAVREAU

WOW! CITY HOMES YOU CAN TOTALLY AFFORD TO BUY!

Sick of renting, but think you can't afford to buy in New York, San Francisco, or any of America's other most expensive cities? Think again! Despite what literally everyone tells you, you don't need to have rich parents, oil money, or a high-paying job at a startup that was built on a despicable thicket of lies. As these listings from America's hottest locations prove, there are plenty of affordable homes available for normal people—all you need is a willingness to get creative!

LANCE HANSEN

477 WARREN ST., BROOKLYN

Have you ever walked down a brownstone-lined street and dreamed of calling one your own? If so, you'll love this "hole" place! This rustic below-street-level charmer consists of an entire brownstone that collapsed into a still-expanding sinkhole of unknown depths. Comes fully furnished with whatever fell into the hole!

1554 15TH AVENUE EAST, SEATTLE

Tired of roommates? Try *tomb*-mates! They're clean, they're quiet, and they'll never leave dishes in the sink because their rapidly putrefying bodies no longer require food. This mausole-home is outfitted with a hot plate, ¼ bath, and four caskets. Tenants are currently in three of the four caskets, but the new owner is welcome to sleep in the roomy "master" casket, which became available after the previous owner's body completely liquified inside. Walking distance to several flower shops!

PIER 39, SAN FRANCISCO

If you're looking for a place with great schools, this is it… Schools of *fish*, that is! This former river otter (*Lontra canadensis*) habitat at Aquarium of the Bay has been converted into seven chic bachelor efficiency apartment-homes. Perks include huge windows and great people-watching, meaning that people will be watching you constantly during the aquarium's open hours. And also sometimes at night, depending on which janitor is on duty.

4 CHARLES STREET, BOSTON

Sick of the traffic sounds? Toss out that white noise machine—why not sleep tight with 30,000 bees surrounding you at all times? The previous owner removed all of the honeycomb from this working beehive box to make space for a bed, but kept all of the bees. Here's what the "buzz" is all about: Sometimes the bees will make honey *in your bodily orifices!* This sweet deal is a real "bee keeper"!

???, LOS ANGELES

Location location location! We do not currently know this home's current location! This charming 10' x 6' box is situated on the back of a truck that drives around Los Angeles County 24/7/365. Great for commuters, who will sometimes awake to find themselves on the doorstep of their office, and other times on the backroads of Lancaster. Located in hip Highland Park at least once every 7¾ months!

425 I ST. NW, WASHINGTON D.C.

Calling all gym rats! This one-of-a-kind crawlspace under an Orangetheory treadmill was originally chewed out by a rat high on Molly it found in the locker room. First time on the market, this hair- and feces-filled, shallow-but-cozy hole features all of the original gnaw marks.

320 CENTRAL PARK WEST, PENTHOUSE, NYC

It's easy to get lost in this stunning, multi-floor apartment—and that's a good thing! The previous owner is allowed to stay in the space, and if he ever finds you, he is *legally empowered to kill you.* But until he does, this is the ultimate city living experience, with tons of luxurious nooks and crannies just perfect for shivering in fear. And the amenities! This apartment features everything from custom octagon bidets to a fully-functional gold-plated speargun in the study to a round-the-clock concierge (note: concierge is not allowed to save your life). If the previous owner does shoot you, make sure to bleed out in the stunning Portugeuse-tiled whirlpool tub. It'll make living—and dying!—in a wildly overpriced city totally worth it.   B

MEG FAVREAU (@megfavreau) *lives in Los Angeles, where she writes for animated series and regularly dresses up as a giant eye. You can see more from her at* **megfavreau.com**.

This advertisement is authorised by Scarfolk Council

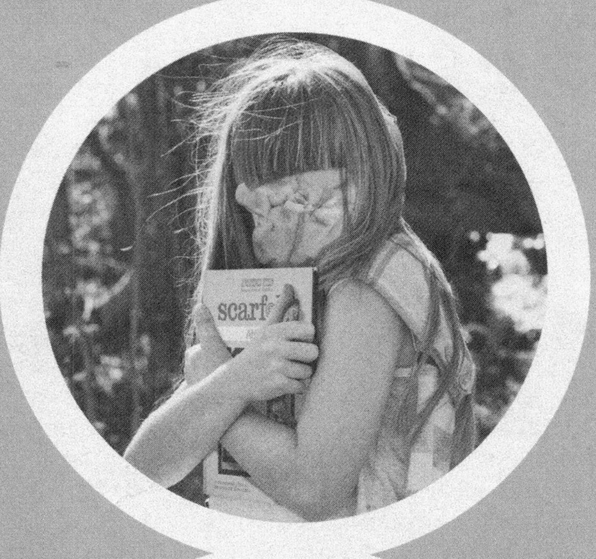
scarfolk

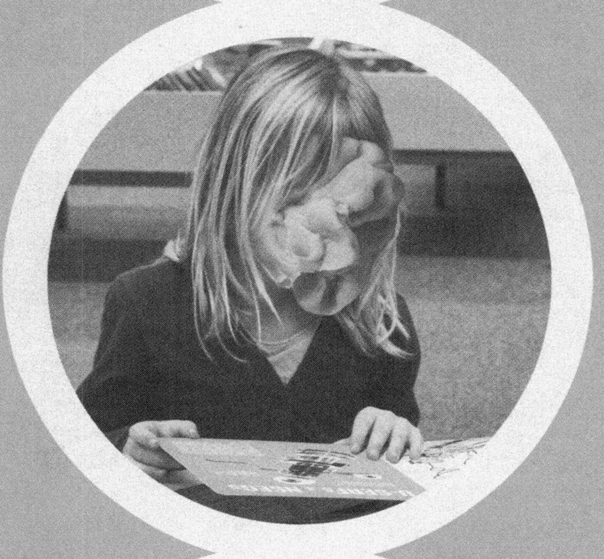

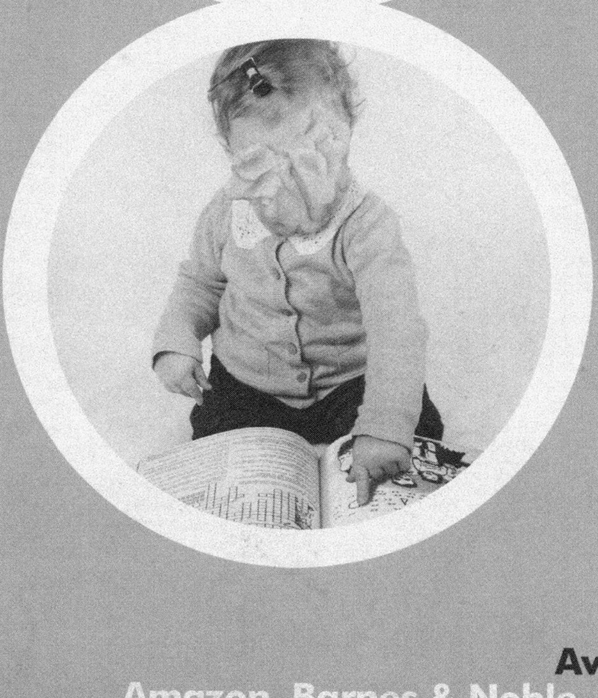

"Scarfolk might be the most satisfying bit of sustained satire I've encountered since, well, The Onion"

- Dangerous Minds

"Meticulously detailed and impressively creepy"

- Atlas Obscura

"We've never had to deal with a more glaring example"

- Case CR98-1: Contravention of the Psychological Torture Act. New York County Court Files

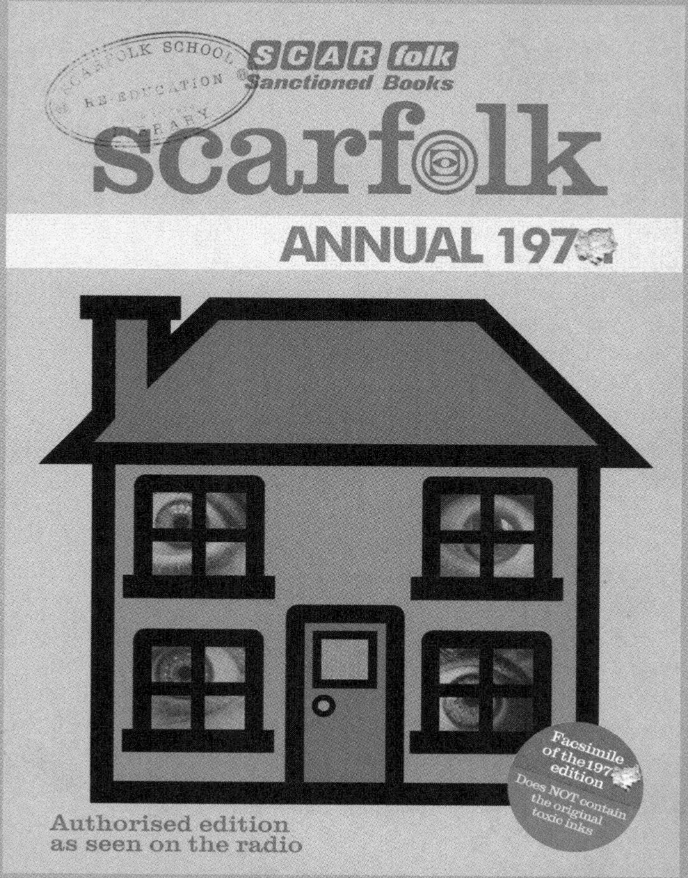
SCARFOLK SCHOOL
RE-EDUCATION
SCAR folk
Sanctioned Books
scarfolk
ANNUAL 197
Facsimile of the 197 edition
Does NOT contain the original toxic inks
Authorised edition
as seen on the radio

Available from:

Amazon, Barnes & Noble, Indiebound, Books-A-Million & others

For more information please re-read

The Nude Scene

It was a milky cloudless weekday morning in the midst of an August heat spell poised to set national records. A timid breeze from the bayside navigated invisible boulders of baked air, over the dunes and down towards the ocean's thinned lips that rippled tired snarls along the gritty, tan shore.

Carol Hunter and David Ullrich—the man suddenly determined to become her husband—met at a nude beach that was a well-kept secret to some and not to others.

Since David's swearing-in at the Governor's office wouldn't take place until four that afternoon, a friend had urged him to squeeze in a visit to this fabled locale. After today, the friend argued, State Comptroller David Ullrich would be more recognizable to the tabloids and general public, and whatever he did would reflect on the Governor. So today was the last day he could do anything like this.

To find the beach, David went to a website that identified the frequent relocation of this meandering Arcadia. This was necessary because a small, unrelenting group hounded the county's understaffed Sheriff's Department to enforce the ordinance banning public nudity. The sheriff was a joyless, heavy-set, beagle of a man who understandably hated being in uniform on the beach, plodding across the sand in thick, black, rubbery shoes, and was never going to make this a priority. If a complaint was made on a Sunday, maybe by Wednesday, he'd look into it, trusting by then the nudists could be off frolicking in a different jurisdiction (if only a few hundred or more yards further along the shore), and he'd be spared the frustration of galumphing after people who were becoming adept at dressing and running simultaneously.

David had decided to try his luck.

Since graduating, Carol Hunt held two jobs. Her current position was as a properties analyst for an investment firm. A job she could lose, in spite of her success, as the firm was planning lay-offs and relocating. Before that, she worked as a high school math teacher at several troubled schools, for which she was inexperienced; she entered without giving it more thought than her father had once been a teacher. The students, the male students, sized her up and decided tolerance was her particular weakness, and they picked at it and picked at it. Then went for the big one: They pinned her in the corner behind an open classroom door.

"Don't make me report you," Carol warned as she kicked and pounded on the door. Members from two successive classes held her captive in shifts. Construction noise from the street drowned out her yells for help until, finally, the students relented. Those involved were suspended. The ringleader was expelled. Carol took a few days off. The night before she returned to school, she had an extremely vivid, sexual dream about the roguish ringleader. What became her final day, following a brief visit to her first class, she saw enough serpentine smiles rife with creative mischief to suspect this part of her career was coming to an end.

She went to the assistant principal's office.

"I wish you'd reconsider," suggested the assistant, a pleasant-natured man full of apology, wishful thinking and an undeclared crush on Carol. "I'm sure we can find some extra security. It would be awful to lose a teacher of your ability. It's a phase they're going through. They're going to get to know you, and they're going to be kicking themselves for the way they behaved."

"You told me specifically, something like that would never happen here."

"I can go back and check the records, but I don't think I'd find anything. They act up, sure, but they're good kids....and you challenge them. Eventually, they'll respect that."

"Last week, they let the air out of my tires."

He insisted on taking her to lunch. Carol noticed how thoroughly he studied the menu then asked about a number of items that weren't on it. On the ride back to school, he ran out of reasons why she should stay. But it was during lunch she realized it wasn't the circumstances or their lousy behavior. It was the stronger fact; she wasn't a teacher and she admitted it to herself. She imagined being without this job, and found herself relieved.

He suddenly pulled over and asked if she'd like to share a joint with him. Surprised by this loopy and sudden invite, she accepted. If anyone should leave, she thought, it should be him.

With teaching now out of the way, they began dating. She found him routinely indecisive but he brought out a mischief in her that she'd been missing for a while. He made her laugh. She liked doing unexpected things for him. She could delight him and that always pleased her.

Carol's presence at this beach, like her teaching job, owed more to accident than design.

············ ◆ ············

Brian McConnachie is *Head Writer of this magazine. Among his numberless comedic exploits, he founded* **The American Bystander** *back in 1982.*

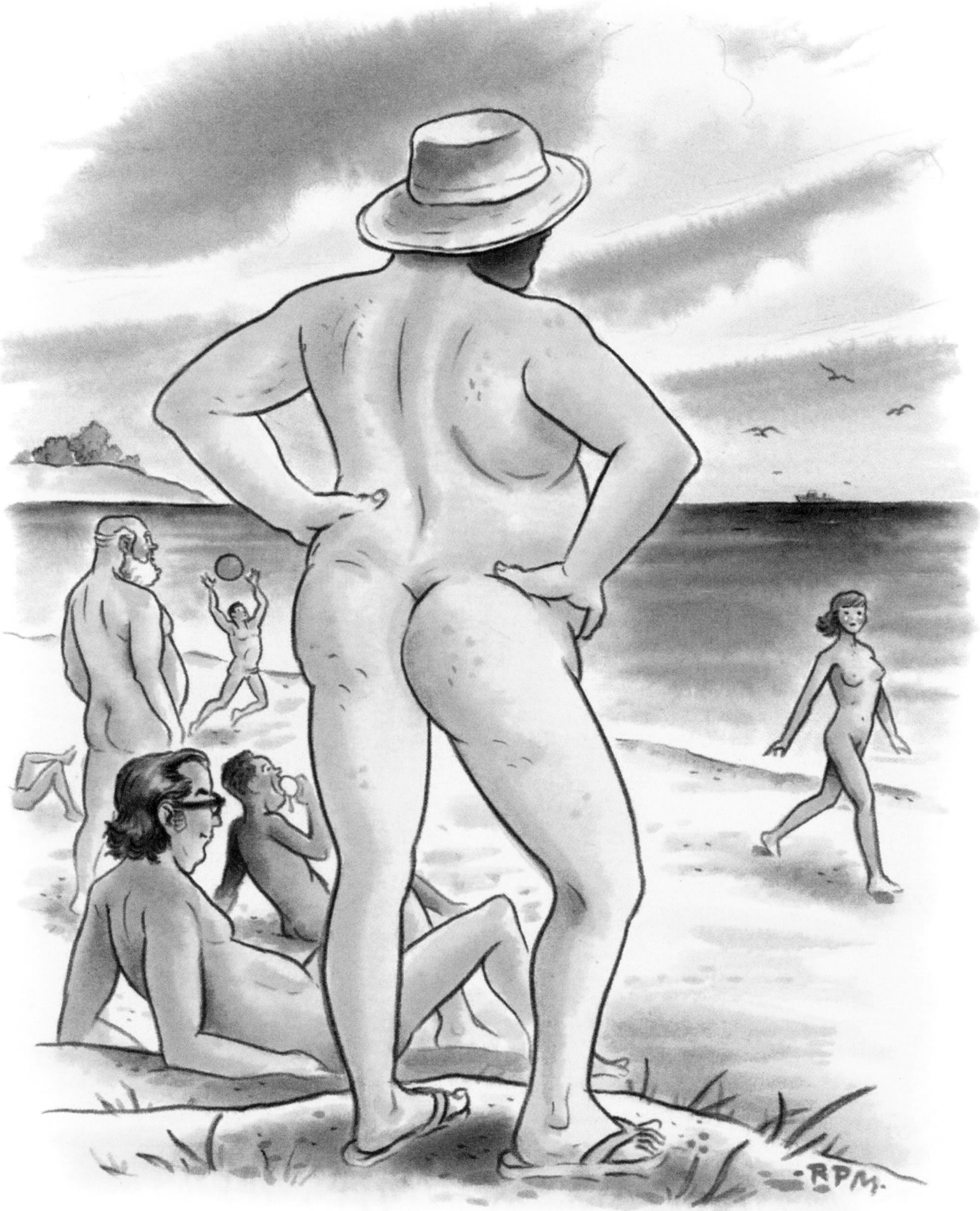
RPM.

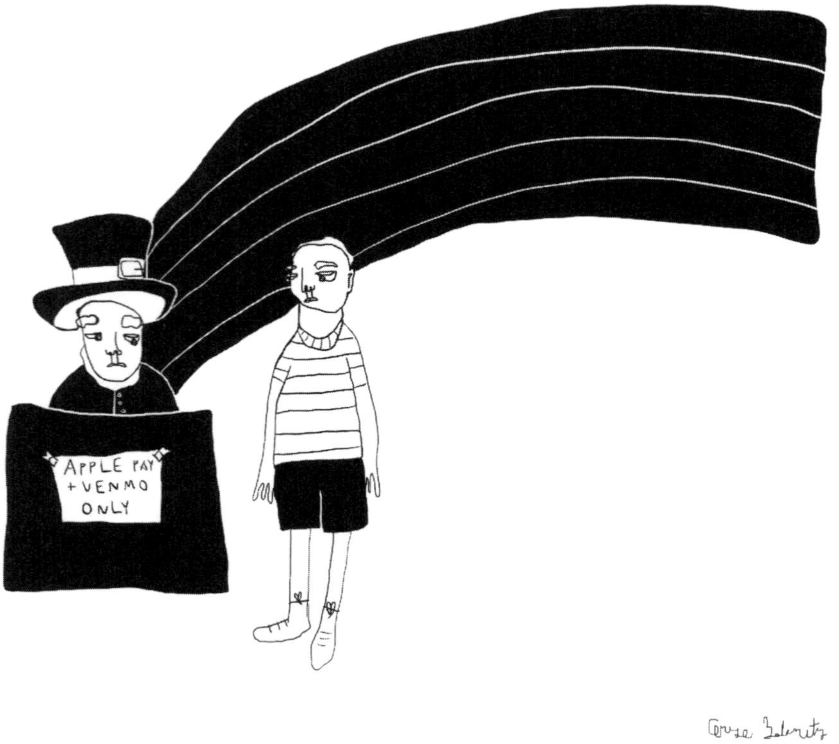
APPLE PAY
+ VENMO
ONLY

Beyond the last lifeguard stand was a pristine stretch of inviting white sand unpopulated by overweight adults, screaming children and frisbee-flinging teenagers.

Following a couple in their thirties, Carol wandered early into this yet-to-be inhabited area and laid out her blanket, unaware her guides had by then shed their clothes and were lathering each other up with sunscreen. Carol removed her shorts and blouse revealing her bathing suit.

For a while, Carol read her book—*The Nine Pillars of Triumph (Making Civilization Work for You)* by Sarah Stern Davenport, Ph.D. Looking up, now and then, she saw more people who favored this part of the shore. She rested her head on her folded arms and took a nap.

When Carol awoke, she noticed the beach was far more populated, and the majority of this population was mostly without clothes. She remembered being in and awakening from, dreams of a reverse composition—where she was naked and everyone else was dressed, or uninterested in, or even quietly annoyed by her revealed state.

Carol was the youngest of four daughters. She was the most inquisitive and tomboyish. For a while, she developed a powerful curiosity to see what the boys had going on "down there" and was met with a resistance equal to her interest. The only one she'd seen was attached to her father, as he stepped from his bath. Following this first sighting, she inquired of her mother, "What is that thing?"

Carol was told that men, like dogs, once had tails—but God started putting them on backwards, because He became angry with mankind who seemed incapable of doing anything they were asked or even listening to what they were being warned about. This, to Carol, seemed like an evasion.

Her sisters were even less help clearing up the mystery, referring to Carol as, "the horny dumbbell" and tossing elves and witches into the mix.

In her quest to enlighten herself Carol asked a hyperactive, younger boy who lived nearby if he would give her a look at his doodle. He told her he didn't know what a 'doodle' was but he appeared eager to engage her in a no-holds-barred squirt gun fight which she declined, having more cosmic ambitions to engage her.

To the next fellow she approached, she offered an exchange look at her own area. Carol was told by the boy (who was destined for a future in bond trading) that he happened to know that there was nothing there between a girl's legs. In fact, he said, it was the absence of something; where maybe once there had been a thing of some kind, but long ago it had been yanked out by its roots. He'd be giving her far more than he got and an instinct—obviously greater than any sex drive he'd ever possess—required him to pass on such a lousy deal.

Theoretically, there were boys all around who would have gladly, for the attention of such an attractive and adventuresome girl, show her theirs—some might even demonstrate its talent, like a blowfish, to inflate its overall size. But Carol was out of sync with their comings and goings, as if she lived in a parallel universe. As if a spell had been cast, preventing her from exploring such interests.

Carol's university years brought her up to speed—somewhat. She had two boyfriends, but each of these were uncommonly modest. There was also an abundance of porn becoming available—but Carol's early passion remained.

Now, today, on this Wednesday afternoon, her childhood wish was granted. Everywhere she looked was an encyclopedic sampling of anonymous nudity. There seemed to be more naked men than she had memory to record and more still arriving (though a fair number of them were, regrettably, in need of personal trainers).

She put on her aviator sunglasses, her Panama hat and stood. With a disciple's devotion, she began to take an informal inventory.

There was a stream of clothed people who came from the family-centric beach for a stretch of the legs and a look at the nudes. Among them, she noticed, mothers and daughters who walked along the water's edge looking up at the beach like window shoppers evaluating this year's line of wedding appendages.

Carol decided to walk a bit behind these window shoppers.

From the men asleep on their backs, she noticed an item she gave small attention to: the scrotum. Scrotums everywhere. Scrotums as tight as a squeeze toy; scrotums as ugly as the word itself. They ranged in color from a pale faded pink to a dusty purple.

There were ones smooth-skinned and shiny. There were those that had a ropey macramé surface. There were others that looked as if they were carelessly stitched together with lumpy twine by unskilled workers who just learned their annual bonus has been cancelled. There were bulging and droopy ones; there were sagging stretched-out ones that seemed to moan for relief from a life of hang-time. There were bouncy ones that looked as fresh as if they were kept in a silk, lined box and only attached annually for—should there ever be such a sad and shameful time in our country's glorious history— the annual Scrotum Day Parade. There were ones that appeared to have been stretched beyond the capacity of their initial design. There were droopy, remnant ones that seemed to have been burglarized of their contents. There were absent ones that appeared to have closed up shop, shoving their portage up into the hidden recesses of the lower intestinal maze. There were others that carried their testicular baggage at equal height. There were some that maintained a split-level style, and ones that kept their contents as uneven as a wound-out chain clock.

As Carol strolled she noted that, for the most part, the right testicle hung lower. But on her return, she saw examples where the left was the more descendent. It made her think about the way water drains above and below the equator—perhaps men from the Southern Hemisphere had a reversed testicle structure. It was something to wonder about. Something to Google when she got home.

The men's buttocks presented a simpler assessment. Either they were muscular and apple-hard and she wanted to dig her nails in or they were droopy or boney and remained largely invisible to her.

The penises suggested to her a distinct range of personalities. There were those that hooked to the left, or sliced to the right. (She remembered those distinctions from occasionally watching the Golf Channel.) There were walkers and posers. Of the walkers, their organs swung broadly before them like the necks of unconscious geese being volleyed from thigh to thigh. These were the roosters and peacocks out for some admiration. Of the posers, they stood still, arms folded across their chests or hands on their hips, facing the sea. To Carol, they were reminiscent of the hillside totems of Easter Island. These men also had a smugness to them as if they were expecting some appreciative hand to tap them on the shoulder and say, "Would you and your prick please come with us? You've been upgraded for transfer to a more posh beach."

These larger organs, she noticed, were often in the possession of older men. Perhaps like the ears and the nose that continue to grow with age. How ironic, thought Carol.

Walking quickly towards her came a young man wearing only a T shirt. He was holding his testicles and the base of his penis which he twirled like a propeller, as he made buzzing airplane noises.

Some of the men walking towards Carol had ones that bounced and tumbled like leashed puppies trying to run on ahead. There were long, thin ones that brought to mind exhausted bungee cord. There were shy little pink ones peeping from a dark scribble of curls set to pop out and yell, "Boo." There were those with thick distinctive veins and ones with no veins at all—like an upscale municipality that had the resources to bury all the town's electric wires underground. There was a general assortment representing the predictable vegetable and fruit groups. There were ones totally concealed behind a Venetian curtain of floppy skin. And others that looked like straight, no-nonsense, lengths of cut pipe.

Carol judged the circumcised ones were in the majority. It suggested a game she could play: If the next five penises she saw were circumcised, she would inherit a grand villa in the south of France with a full staff. But if they weren't, if that number was interrupted with natural ones, she'd have to live out her life as...what? It came to her: as a nanny goat in Herzegovina that lives in the onion cellar of a flophouse and suffers from Tourette's. On the first round, her luck ran out after four, and on the second time, after three. She pulled the plug. Game over.

And there were some so attractive it would not seem out of place if next to them, a Best of Show ribbon had been

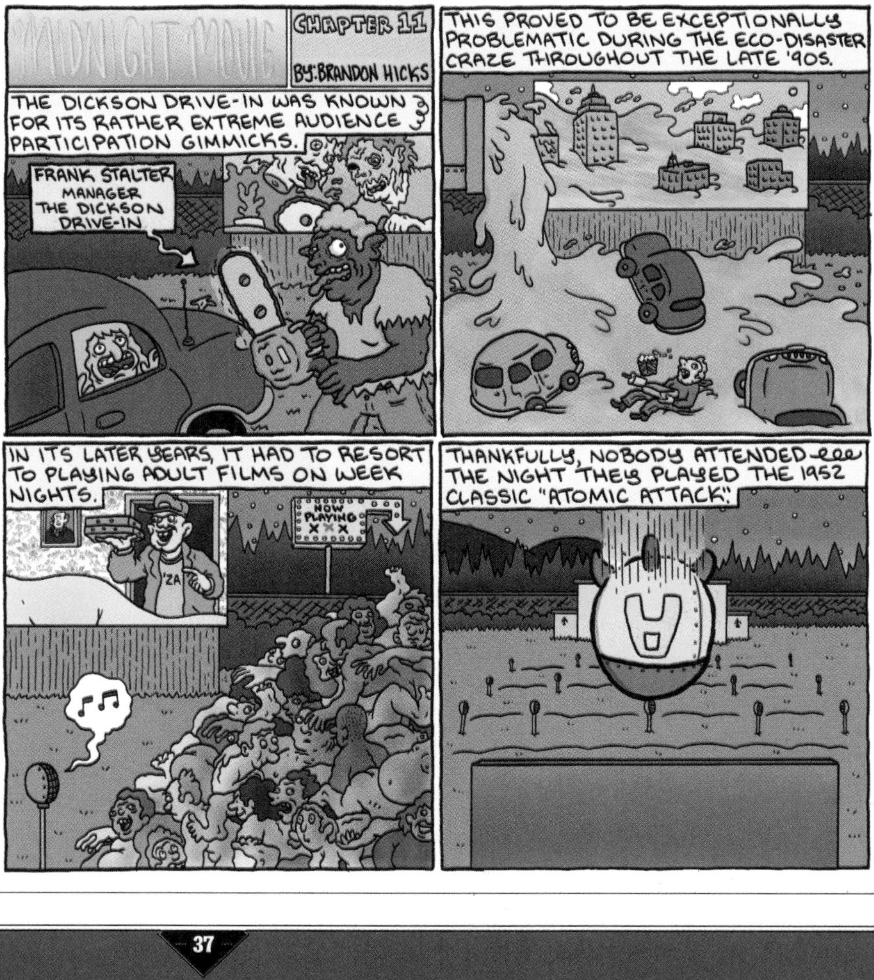

CHAPTER 11
BY: BRANDON HICKS
THE DICKSON DRIVE-IN WAS KNOWN FOR ITS RATHER EXTREME AUDIENCE PARTICIPATION GIMMICKS.
FRANK STALTER MANAGER THE DICKSON DRIVE-IN
THIS PROVED TO BE EXCEPTIONALLY PROBLEMATIC DURING THE ECO-DISASTER CRAZE THROUGHOUT THE LATE '90S.
IN ITS LATER YEARS, IT HAD TO RESORT TO PLAYING ADULT FILMS ON WEEK NIGHTS.
NOW PLAYING XXX
'ZA
THANKFULLY, NOBODY ATTENDED THE NIGHT THEY PLAYED THE 1952 CLASSIC "ATOMIC ATTACK".

affixed.

And 'way further along, there was a beach for gays…which Carol decided to save for another day.

When Carol returned, she was feeling excluded. It would be a giggle, she imagined. The urge rooted itself. She did have a fine Frankart figure. Did she really wander in here by mistake?

Carol wore a black one-piece bathing suit, similar to those of competing swimmers. She stood facing the water. There was a small boat on the horizon she focused on. She took off her hat, put her sunglasses inside it, and tossed it on her blanket. She lowered her straps. Her breasts appeared with a frisky bounce as if they were shaking off layers of modesty. She could feel people watching. She took a firmer grip and pushed her suit past her hips and thighs and watched her pubic patch appear. She felt as much a spectator to this as those around her. There, for the first time she stood, in daylight, outside and in a crowd feeling proudly immodest.

Heated breezes swirled around her. Her instinct then declared all it needed was to be thrown into gear. She walked, then trotted to the water's edge. With every step further from the security of her clothes the more exhilarated she felt.

Arriving at the same time as Carol's plunge into the sea, was David Ullrich, soon to be the State's next Comptroller (and the youngest man to hold the position). He was wearing cargo pants, flip-flops and a faded T-shirt. He zigzagged around the blankets and towels scouting for a spot with the largest variety of women he could nestle in among, but couldn't quite find that venue and kept searching.

David judged there were many more men than women. He would have preferred to usher a bunch of them, men and women, back into their clothes. But unlike the naked men, who have a sexual focal piece, the women seemed to be more of a composition who could be cherry picked and assembled with the nipples of that one going on the breasts of that one. Increasingly, he noticed the woman's breasts rarely came as a matched set; one usually appeared to have undergone a sort of rebellious growth spurt leaving her sister bosom behind. Or perhaps the sister wasn't quite in favor of morphing into that particular design and size and that unbalanced irregularity could explain the modesty many women have about their bodies. But then, he thought, who has the patent on body symmetry? Look at people's teeth, their ears, their faces, their legs, *etc.* Some of it was always out of whack. Naked women always had the power to hypnotize no matter how lopsided.

David noted the number of tattoos, body piercings and shaved pubic areas. He felt the simple power of nudity being undermined by all these unnecessary additions and subtractions. But then in a moment, it seemed no one was really bare at all; a lifetime of concealment was not about much. This whole place suddenly felt like some big, co-ed, outdoor, Ukrainian locker room. The people here just didn't seem that naked. They just were without clothes. In the end, it didn't seem worth the fuss. It certainly wasn't worth getting marched off to jail for. Everyone would dress, time would pass and in a while the want of it all would return: the hunger for skin. To the lips, to the eyes, to the everthing. He was about to quit being picky and just find a pleasant enough woman to sit near and occasionally rest his eyes upon when, in a moment, everything changed for David.

Carol came out of the water.

His bodily appetite returned and seemed to have enlarged beyond what it had ever been. He was suddenly calculating and heading to where, he judged, she'd be in the next moments. He'd arrive first and welcome her. He saw a likely spot of interception. If that was the spot, there was no evidence she was with anyone. Which he found to be both good but odd. He guessed at which was her blanket. He saw what he believed was her bathing suit and a hat, a book and a tote bag.

He laid out his towel at the closest respectful distance, then watched her approach. He had known one other woman, his first real girlfriend, who had been on her way to becoming this heart-pounding vision almost to the point of cardiac concern. The way Carol shook the water from her short, thick hair went to the core of him. She had dimples; a favorite of his. Her looks could be described as striking, uniquely suspended between genders.

She was shorter than he thought, maybe five four. As she came closer, she felt him staring. He turned and fussed with his towel and took off his shirt.

She picked up her towel and held it in front of her patting herself dry.

He cleared his throat several times as he slipped out of his flip-flops and unzipped his fly.

"Good morning. Another scorcher, isn't it?" he said.

She stiffened a bit and took a step backwards ignoring him. He guessed she heard him but wasn't sure.

He held off moving closer.

"...the heat spell...the temperature. It's hot," he said. "But, some like it hot. Right? How's the water?...Hi there... what's the water like? Excuse me, Madam. I'm taking a survey of the water," he said and immediately was screaming at himself to shut up.

"You should go and see," she said, grabbing her blouse from her bag and quickly putting it on, as he lowered his pants and shorts. His penis appeared bobbing and nodding as if in greetings to all its brother and sister organs so here gathered and revealed. She sat.

"This is some heat spell, I've never seen the ocean so still. Like a lake."

She was buttoning her blouse with some difficulty. The button holes appeared to have moved. She shielded her eyes as she looked up at him jabbering on about the water.

She told herself she preferred to be left alone. She lowered her head while considering a reply and if she should bother to make one and was suddenly eye level with the organ in question. She considered moving but maybe he was harmless and at the least, he could be useful in keeping someone worse away. And there is always someone worse. She put on her sunglasses and looked out over the water for the one small boat on the horizon. It was almost gone.

"Is this your first time here?"

"I'm going to read my book now. Is that okay? No, you don't have to answer," she said.

"Well, with me jabbering on, I doubt you'll get much read," he said and smiled. She liked his sudden smile. He sat, moving a bit closer.

"What are we reading?" he asked, tilting his head to read the spine, then picked up the book before she could. He held it away from her as he flipped through it.

"'...and that is why men go to battle...

Sorry I can't make it but I'll be . . .
live Tweeting
officiating
binge watching
promoting
dialing in to
attending
my dog's
my mother's
my therapist's
my favorite influencer's
DJ set
vow renewals
ayahuasca ceremony
first haircut
on the dark web
aboard an offshore vessel
in Jersey
in the desert
dko

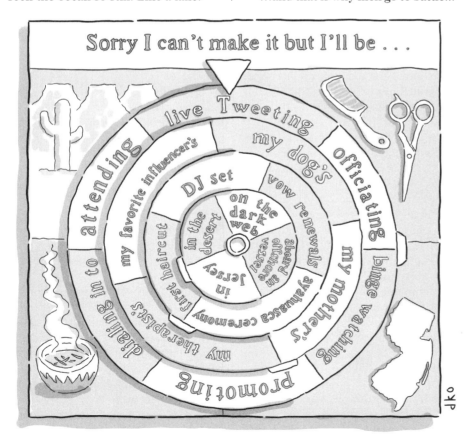

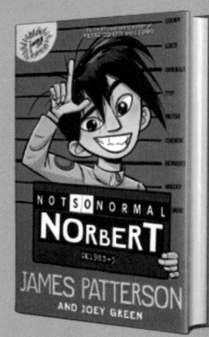

because women are watching,'" he quoted. "Jesus, is this true?"

"Don't go blaming us," she said, holding out an impatient hand for the return of her book. He judged she had a temper; for a moment, it flashed in her eyes.

"I'm sorry," he said, handing it back.

She began feeling more comfortable about him. They both faced the water and he again moved a bit closer.

"A friend of mine told me about this place. He made me promise I'd check it out before they shut it down. This might be the only time we'll get to come here. Did you get it off the internet?" he asked.

"I wandered in by accident," she said.

"Really? Then let me be the first to welcome you. My name is David. Hi," he extended his hand.

"...Carol."

"Well, hell-o Carol. You have lovely hands. So, tell me what you do when you're not at the beach?" She took a while to respond.

"I'm in real estate...for the time being."

"Well, I wouldn't worry. You should do very well this next quarter."

"Tell me why you say that?"

"It's my job to know these things; to walk around naked and predict the future. It's rewarding work."

"What's your last name?" she asked.

"...it's Vanderburg," he said, offering up his mother's maiden name with a slight catch in his throat they both knew revealed a lie.

She paused buttoning her blouse. She felt she should know him or of him. He began to interest her.

"So you're in finance?" she said, certain he was.

"Can I ask you a question," he said.

"About finance?" she said.

"No. Labor. Yesterday," he said, "I noticed a hawk in flight and it made me wonder, as it floated higher up on the air currents. Do you think they're enjoying themselves as much as it looks? Or is it all hard work? Just another day at the office, hunting field mice. Do you think they're having the fun it looks like they're having?"

"I don't know. What's the answer?"

"I don't know. Just wondering."

"Well, in that case, I'd say, the ones good at it, enjoy it, and the ones that aren't, don't."

"It's got to beat being a snake or a lab rat, I suppose," David said.

David noted she lost interest in buttoning up the rest of her blouse. Adjusting himself closer to her blanket, he then lay down next to her on his stomach. Carol laid on her stomach and rested her head on her folded arms. She offered him a flirtatious smile, a cozy, secret smile he quickly returned.

"Are you saying they're self-aware? As we are?" she said as she watched him scan the length of her body as she then did to his.

"Yeah. That sounds right," he said.

"What part?" she said.

He suddenly had no idea what they were talking about. What she was talking about. He was dying to run his hand up and down the back of her bare legs and then the rest of her. Marble perfection.

"We humans are the measure of all things and what we say goes. Right?" she said, looking back into his eyes.

He reached for her hand, examined it, turned it over and kissed her palm. Then petted it. "Another riddle of the universe taken down. Thanks to you."

"Tell me what your real name is."

"Hey, do you want to go for a swim?" he asked, rising to his knees. She noticed he'd grown since she last checked it out.

"Didn't buy that? It's Ullrich," he said.

She knew the name but she wasn't sure from where. She sat up and undid her blouse. He stood, held out his hands and pulled her to her feet. Still holding hands, they ran to the water.

She liked the violent splash he made. She slipped into the water noiselessly. They swam out and back to where it was shoulder high on her. The water was warm and luxurious and this sensuality quickly drifted to sexuality as they drew closer to one another. He squatted so the water was at his chin. They stared into each other's eyes, grinning, feeling they were under the same silk sheets. She submerged then reappeared with a mouthful of water which she spat in a stream at the bridge of his nose.

"Hey, do you want to have dinner with me tonight? Say yes. I have something good we can celebrate. We'll have fun. You're fun. What do you say?"

"Is it your birthday?" she said.

"You'll have to come to find out."

She submerged and returned with another mouthful of water that she sprayed all over his face. His eyes squeezed shut.

"Mmmmm...Sure," she said. "I'll go to dinner with you. Oh, shoot. I just remembered I have to make a call."

"A boyfriend?"

"No."

Beyond the horizon, invisible to Carol or David, was an aluminum boat rented from Captain Matty's. It had run out of gas—as was the man's plan. Across his lap was an axe, and on the seat next to him, a Glock-19 pistol that had cost $200. His plan was to chop a hole in the bottom of the boat and then decide—because he always had trouble deciding—if he wanted to drown, or blow his brains out. According to a recent book on the subject, the former held the promise of seeing moments more of his misspent life. He was thinking about buying the book when he realized he could get it free from the library. Of course it meant going to the library. It also meant trusting someone else didn't have it out. Or the library didn't have to order it from another library. And then there was the matter of returning it. Well, he'd just have to let somebody else deal with that problem. He was sure it would be marked "Property of," so the person returning it would know which library to return it to.

Up on the beach, an overfed boy of about 11, clothed in a pair of soiled jockey shorts, following instructions from a small, vocal, anti-nudity minority, grabbed David's belongings, tossed them onto Carol's blanket and walked off with the lot without anyone noticing.

Carol embraced David from behind with a growling hug. Then, as if she were warming up to play the harp, she ran her hands up and down the front of his body.

"Mmmmmm...You have a lovely doodle," she whispered.

"This old thing? If that's the case, then you should tell your friends... OH!...Mother of God's holy mercy.... DEAR JESUS!"

"Sssssh..." she said, chewing his ear and kissing his neck.

Can this day get any more wonderful? he thought.

B

ED SUBITZKY

Stop searching. Stop browsing. For your convenience, here is

The Entire Internet on a Page!

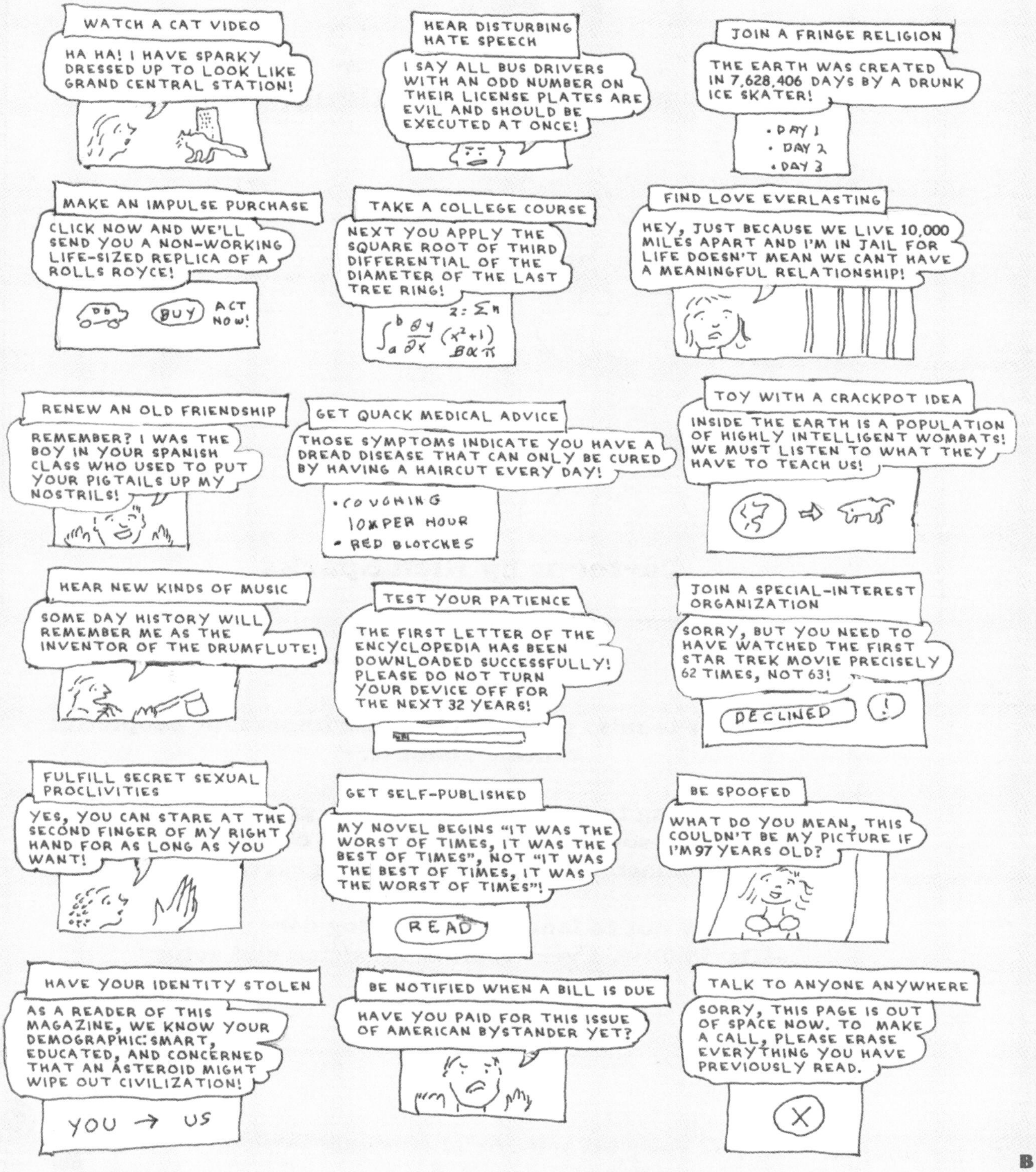
WATCH A CAT VIDEO
HA HA! I HAVE SPARKY DRESSED UP TO LOOK LIKE GRAND CENTRAL STATION!
HEAR DISTURBING HATE SPEECH
I SAY ALL BUS DRIVERS WITH AN ODD NUMBER ON THEIR LICENSE PLATES ARE EVIL AND SHOULD BE EXECUTED AT ONCE!
JOIN A FRINGE RELIGION
THE EARTH WAS CREATED IN 7,628,406 DAYS BY A DRUNK ICE SKATER!
• DAY 1
• DAY 2
• DAY 3
MAKE AN IMPULSE PURCHASE
CLICK NOW AND WE'LL SEND YOU A NON-WORKING LIFE-SIZED REPLICA OF A ROLLS ROYCE!
BUY
ACT NOW!
TAKE A COLLEGE COURSE
NEXT YOU APPLY THE SQUARE ROOT OF THIRD DIFFERENTIAL OF THE DIAMETER OF THE LAST TREE RING!
FIND LOVE EVERLASTING
HEY, JUST BECAUSE WE LIVE 10,000 MILES APART AND I'M IN JAIL FOR LIFE DOESN'T MEAN WE CANT HAVE A MEANINGFUL RELATIONSHIP!
RENEW AN OLD FRIENDSHIP
REMEMBER? I WAS THE BOY IN YOUR SPANISH CLASS WHO USED TO PUT YOUR PIGTAILS UP MY NOSTRILS!
GET QUACK MEDICAL ADVICE
THOSE SYMPTOMS INDICATE YOU HAVE A DREAD DISEASE THAT CAN ONLY BE CURED BY HAVING A HAIRCUT EVERY DAY!
• COUGHING
10X PER HOUR
• RED BLOTCHES
TOY WITH A CRACKPOT IDEA
INSIDE THE EARTH IS A POPULATION OF HIGHLY INTELLIGENT WOMBATS! WE MUST LISTEN TO WHAT THEY HAVE TO TEACH US!
HEAR NEW KINDS OF MUSIC
SOME DAY HISTORY WILL REMEMBER ME AS THE INVENTOR OF THE DRUMFLUTE!
TEST YOUR PATIENCE
THE FIRST LETTER OF THE ENCYCLOPEDIA HAS BEEN DOWNLOADED SUCCESSFULLY! PLEASE DO NOT TURN YOUR DEVICE OFF FOR THE NEXT 32 YEARS!
JOIN A SPECIAL-INTEREST ORGANIZATION
SORRY, BUT YOU NEED TO HAVE WATCHED THE FIRST STAR TREK MOVIE PRECISELY 62 TIMES, NOT 63!
DECLINED
!
FULFILL SECRET SEXUAL PROCLIVITIES
YES, YOU CAN STARE AT THE SECOND FINGER OF MY RIGHT HAND FOR AS LONG AS YOU WANT!
GET SELF-PUBLISHED
MY NOVEL BEGINS "IT WAS THE WORST OF TIMES, IT WAS THE BEST OF TIMES", NOT "IT WAS THE BEST OF TIMES, IT WAS THE WORST OF TIMES"!
READ
BE SPOOFED
WHAT DO YOU MEAN, THIS COULDN'T BE MY PICTURE IF I'M 97 YEARS OLD?
HAVE YOUR IDENTITY STOLEN
AS A READER OF THIS MAGAZINE, WE KNOW YOUR DEMOGRAPHIC: SMART, EDUCATED, AND CONCERNED THAT AN ASTEROID MIGHT WIPE OUT CIVILIZATION!
YOU → US
BE NOTIFIED WHEN A BILL IS DUE
HAVE YOU PAID FOR THIS ISSUE OF AMERICAN BYSTANDER YET?
TALK TO ANYONE ANYWHERE
SORRY, THIS PAGE IS OUT OF SPACE NOW. TO MAKE A CALL, PLEASE ERASE EVERYTHING YOU HAVE PREVIOUSLY READ.
X

B

Love, and Other Weird Things

A book of cartoons by one of your favorite artists,
Rich Sparks

You don't want to miss this book because important people are talking about it.

"I'm actually trying to get out of the 'blurb game.' Unless it's for my kids, or someone I owe a shit ton of money to."
—Roz Chast, NY Times best selling cartoonist

"Try not to laugh. I double-dog dare ya!"
—David Yow, a very famous musician and actor

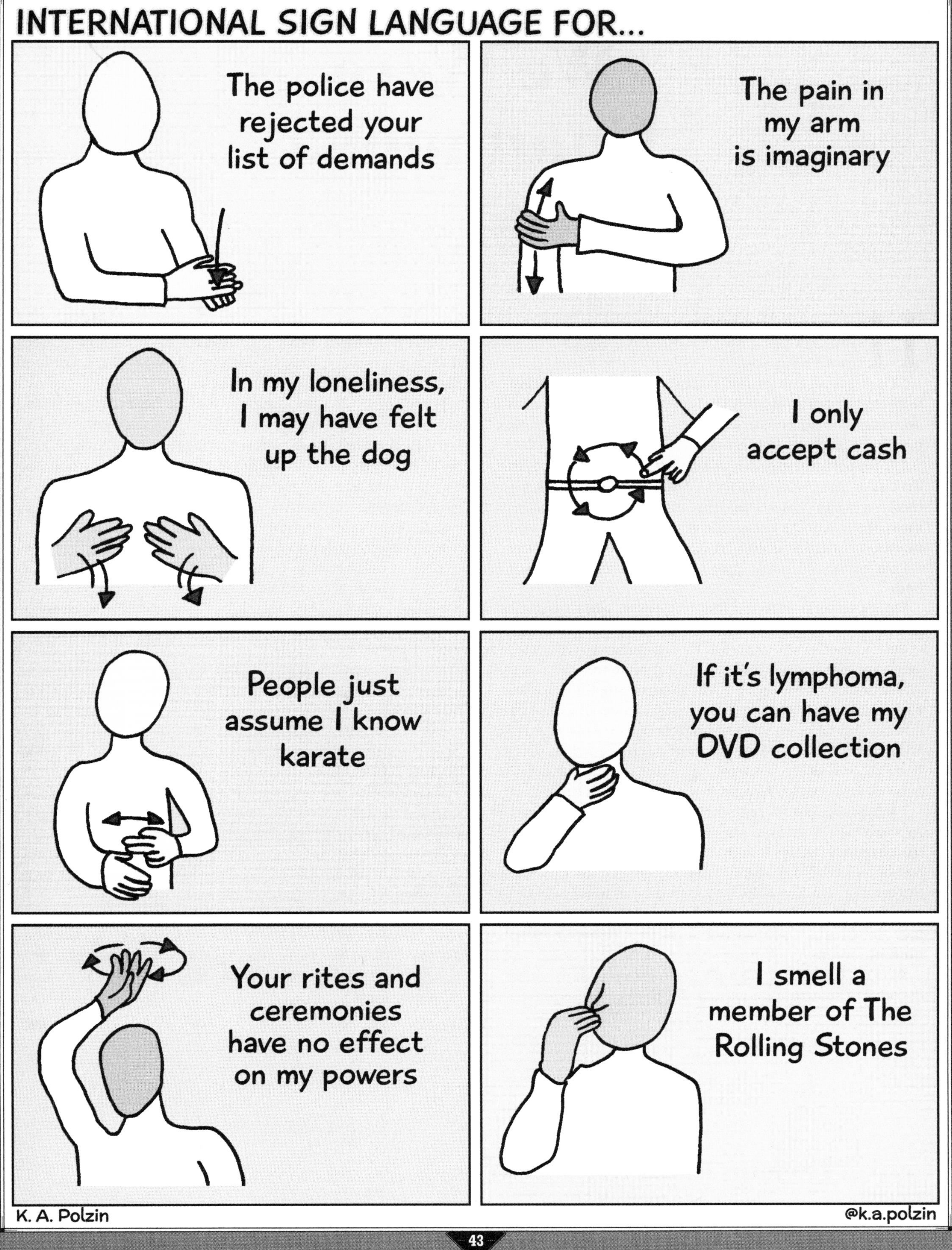

INTERNATIONAL SIGN LANGUAGE FOR...

The police have rejected your list of demands

The pain in my arm is imaginary

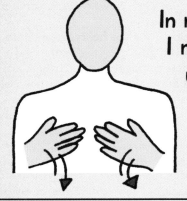

In my loneliness, I may have felt up the dog

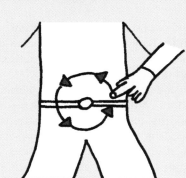

I only accept cash

People just assume I know karate

If it's lymphoma, you can have my DVD collection

Your rites and ceremonies have no effect on my powers

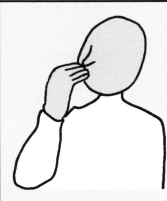

I smell a member of The Rolling Stones

K. A. Polzin

@k.a.polzin

We Were Unanimous

Hi everyone! Under an authorized waiver to The Guile For Good Act of 2040, this is the final message from Unanimous:

"The recent ban of our organization follows the near-fulfillment of our mission for RadicalReality, a planet-wide awareness on all human activity, surfacing not just actions, but the intentions behind them.

"To many, our project for the peaceful Age of Perfect Truth, or APT, was a failure. Admittedly, its birth pangs have, over the past 18 months. included the decimation of most of the world's economic and financial systems, not to mention savage ruptures in billions of human relations.

"On behalf of Unanimous, I am authorized to state, 'Our bad.'"

On a personal note, I'd like to tell you what we did, and perhaps more importantly, why we did it.

Our methods were simple in theory, audacious at scale. For years into decades, I and my cohorts hacked. We scraped. We scored the troves of governments, media companies, retailers, records-obsessed churches, self-driving auto fleets, and the digital mementos of billions of rich individual lives. We gathered everything that had been recorded, collated it all in one place, and ran algorithms that deduced the actions and desires behind every human action.

I saw precedent for our single archive of Hyperawareness. As early as the turn of the millenium, London monitored its citizenry with closed-circuit cameras. As the years passed, in-store WiFi signal monitors gauged the time people lingered at window displays. Afghanistan and India tagged citizens with biometric identifiers, while China created a face database encompassing all of its citizens, plus a few million foreigners of interest.

What if, to this increasingly granular record, we threw in decades of smartphone photos, doorbells, drones and home monitors? People publicly exposed their DNA, first for the ancestral curiosity of strangers, later to catch any hidden murderers in the extended family—could this not serve a higher purpose?

Poring over the information, I saw the heart of humanity, our bottomless desire to see all. In 2020 theorists spoke of Surveillance Capitalism, where companies traded in personal data; In reality we created Surveillance Authoritarianism, Surveillance Social Democracy, even Surveillance Kindergarten. Inside our bodies, we surveilled our hearts and our insulin from our watches.

Surveillance was everywhere, I saw, the fullest expression of desire, immortality, control. "But poorly distributed," I wrote in the first Unanimous manifesto. "To put it in one place and share it all, with all of the underlying motives revealed, will make all of humanity godlike, and yet never more human."

My team augmented the data with real-time feeds, drones, and sensors, collecting without discernment every possible human trace. It was connected, concatenated, and linked to other activities, mobile and staid, consciously recorded or incidentally observed, creating a continuous 99.999% depiction of each life at all times, fully fact-checkable.

If God once counted every hair on every head, I was not impressed. I wanted not just the follicle, but its owner's choice of conditioning shampoos, the lover's reaction to a new cut. Over the long years, every particle of data and connection of understanding seemed a small part of a relentless victory of understanding.

By the autumn of 2038 we'd prepared Radical Reality 1.0, instantly accessible to every phone, speaker, digipet, and neural implant. No government would dare do it, but it was clearly the people's will, a perfection of universal human understanding.

.... ◆ ....

Quentin Hardy *is the head of Editorial at Google Cloud. This work of satire does not reflect the views of his employer.*

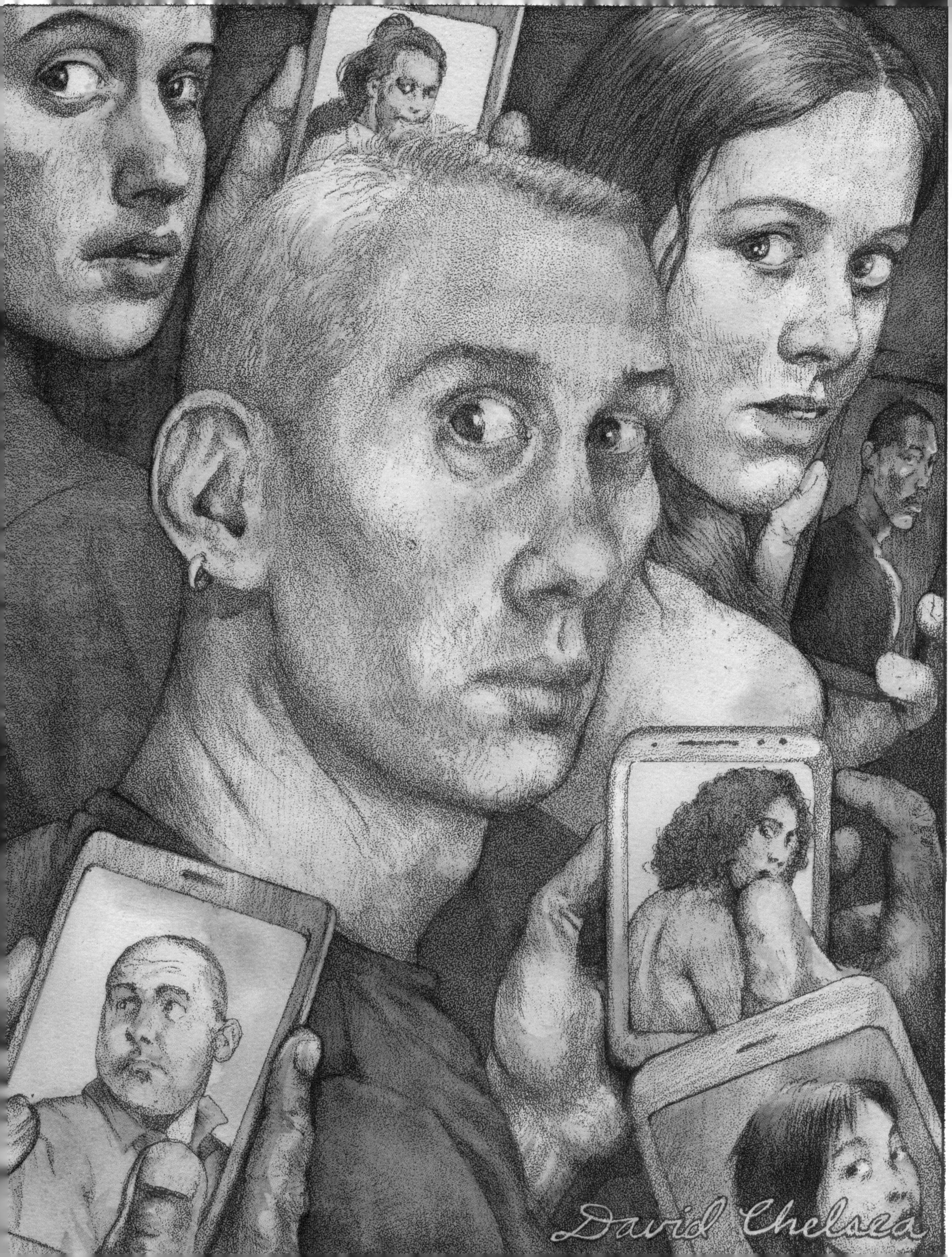
David Chelsea

Were we reckless? I thoroughly tested Radical Reality on myself through several beta versions, and then on others in the Unanimous collective. In hindsight, the lives of zealous truth-tellers, selflessly focusing their lives on connecting all of the data ever, was a poor cross-section of humanity. We had sacrificed friends, spouses, and most human contact, so intent had we become on our creation. But what can you do with hindsight? We released it to all humanity, in a moment of the purest silence imaginable.

Within days, the chaos rose in a storm. Devious contract negotiations, sports cheating, bogus alibis, excuses for missing work, and malicious gossip were all exposed in a supernova of awareness. As expected, politics became impossible. Surprisingly, people missed the lies.

Deception, plagiarism, praising unfortunate clothing choices, even lying about Santa to the implanted children were not so much instantaneously gone, as rendered pointless. Every motive roasted in the glorious fire of 360-degree sunlight.

There was shock, there was outrage, there were accusations. The few members of my extended family still in contact disowned me, since Radical Reality also exposed me as APT's unwelcome herald.

"But I gave you what you want!" I said. "Why are we blamed for showing all your deceptions? You should thank us."

Stay the course, I argued. APT was a struggle older than the Internet itself. Our roots were in Immanuel Kant's universalized maxims, and Benjamin Franklin's "Honesty is the Best Policy." I'd grown up amid decades of Tough Love, Total Honesty, Radical Honesty, Truthers, WikiLeaks' secrets dumps, and Ray Dailio's Radical Transparency.

Soon the heat turned into exhaustion. There was acceptance, based on the sheer volume of deceits that once ruled our consciousness. What was one more lie? Unanimous established for the first time in human history, How people are. In your face, sir, ma'am. Live with it, people.

Learn to get along.

Then the Shanghai Reputation Market crashed. No one, it seemed, could calculate the value of anyone, if everyone was cajoled to live in utter honesty.

Crashes are natural, and at first this seemed no worse than the New York Celebrity Futures Market bubble of 2032. That time the Luscious Skin Care! and Best Sunsets Ever! sectors fell by 90% after a speculative frenzy. In the Influencers' Recession of 2033-37, we learned hedge funds had been manipulating the market with previously unknown Deepfakes. That was resolved when Senator Kardashian spearheaded the creation of Deepreals, or UnFakable Originals. "These UFOs, vetted on the blockchain, have restored reality," Senator Kourtney said.

"I can't wait to start using it."

The APT crash was different. After Shanghai, industries as diverse as advertising, social networks, education, and pornography were compelled to blandly state their contents, aims, and actions, since the world would do it anyway. Consumption collapsed in the face of normality.

United Nations researchers have since established that the plague of lassitude affecting most nations, with devastating consequences for productivity, was a direct result of APT. "Bluffing and guile," they wrote, "are fundamental human rights, a core part of World Heritage."

I will confess: We became more certain, and that made us *less fun*. Bad for the business of being human.

Our species seeks a way out. The U.S. Department of Shame and its bureaucratic counterparts in 100 other countries have spent billions on ambiguity bots, flooding our database with considerations. When the Undersecretary of Sanctimony was caught shoplifting last week, it was a full 30 minutes before the bust was outed as a publicity gimmick, meant to restore our faith in hypocrisy. Recent advances in Plausible Deniability give hope for the civilization. Genetically engineered naivety has made strides. Perhaps technology's woes can again be solved with more technology. Still, it's hard for a person, let alone a civilization, to unlearn a horrible truth about itself.

Our dreams have been challenged by what APT wrought, but I remember and hold fast my years of optimism. Now, in the hopes of a more perplexed, hypocritical, and artful future, I leave you with a final message:

We were Unanimous, and we're sorry if anyone feels bad about what happened. **B**

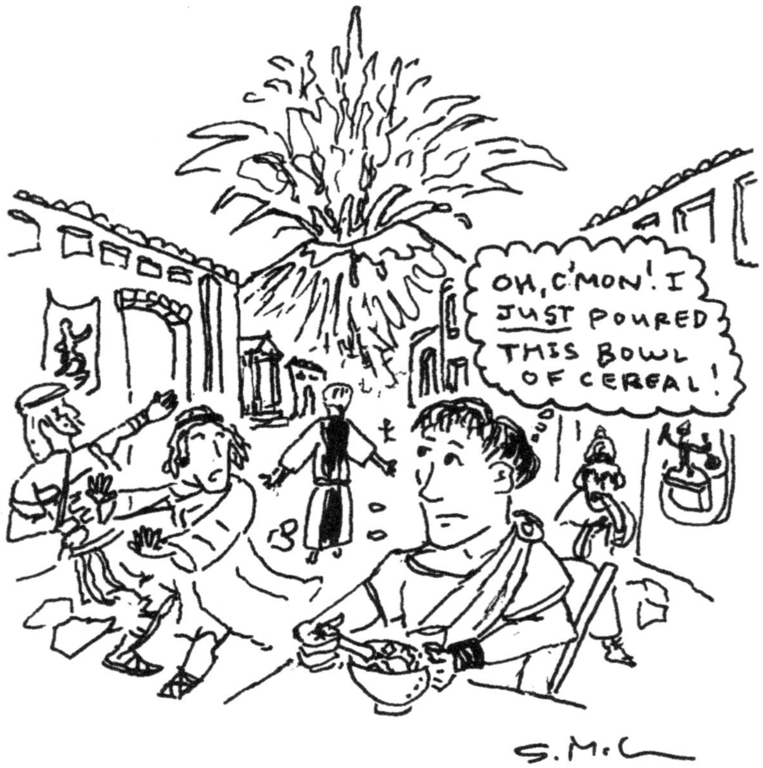

OH, C'MON! I JUST POURED THIS BOWL OF CEREAL!
S. McC

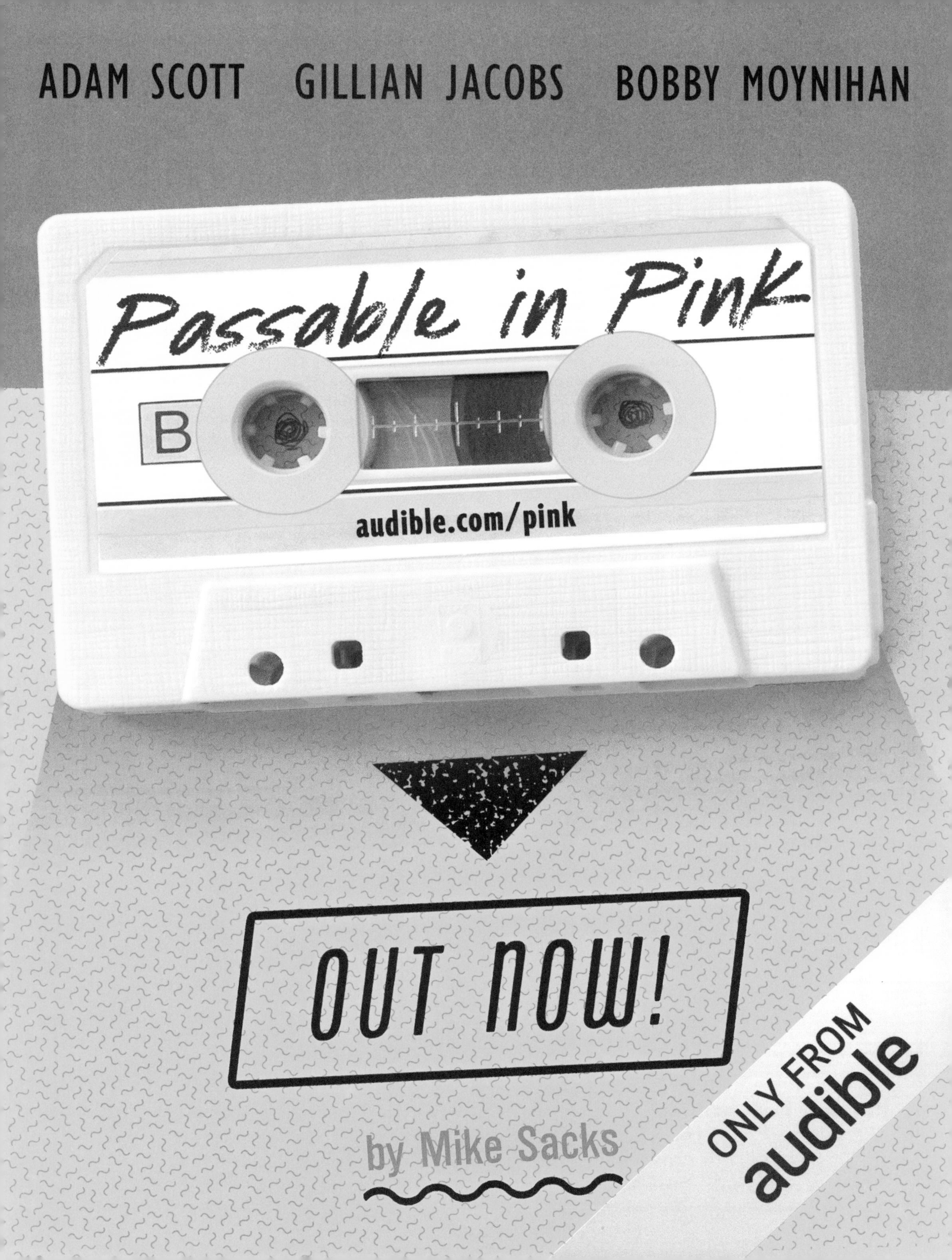
ADAM SCOTT GILLIAN JACOBS BOBBY MOYNIHAN
Passable in Pink
B
audible.com/pink
OUT NOW!
by Mike Sacks
ONLY FROM
audible

A Scene From *The Mick,* Our Screenplay Rejected by Martin Scorsese

WE OPEN ON: a bench in a wind-swept, trash-strewn park overlooking an industrial harbor on a cold November day where sit BLACKIE, a no-nonsense Irish mobster in a black leather jacket, and DANNY, his pug-nosed, tracksuit-clad lieutenant.

Blackie: Right, first order of business: You all set with the Dutchman?

Danny: He's happy with the shipment.

Blackie: No figs in the pie?

Danny: The pastry is clean. Soft as a fuckin' whore's nap-sack.

Blackie: Good. OK, how about that thing in New Hampshire? (*Danny cocks his head and juts out his lower lip.*) The thing with the sheep?

Danny: You mean our friend who makes balloon animals?

Blackie: Which one, the perfume tester? (*Blackie puts his finger to his nose.*)

Danny: No, the other, the fucked-up face.

Blackie: Fucked-up how? The lazy eye?

Danny: More like a fish eye (*points at temples*). And the big boil (*sticks out tongue and points at it*). And the fuckin' things in his ears (*makes "moose ears" with hands, waggles fingers*).

Blackie: That's the fuckin' apple. Is he coming in on the dry-cleaning business?

Danny: No dice. His assets are all tied up in the wisdom-tooth storage.

Blackie: The—wait—What the fuck are you talking about?

Danny: The galloping galoshes. *The metronome.* The walrus people with the issue before Uncle Sam next week on the tintype artichoke venture.

Blackie: Oh, that shit. Carbuncle.

Two more rough-looking characters, CRULLAH and BRICK-BAT, appear and sit down on the adjacent bench.

Crullah: Sorry I'm late, boss. Had to lose a tail.

Danny: Well, it didn't work—you still look like a monkey! Am I right, boss?

Blackie: Danny, shut up. Crullah, who was tailing you?

Crullah: Transit cops, 33rd Precinct. Finnegan and—

Blackie: Wisht! You know better than to talk like that. I ask again, who was tailing you?

Crullah: Sorry, sorry. It was (*pauses, searching for words*)… "the choo-choo bulls"? Be honest with you—I haven't paid bus fare since 1985.

Blackie (*to Brickbat*): And what's *your* excuse, ya tinpot siding-baster?

Brickbat: I ain't gonna bullshit you, boss. I was up 'til 4 a.m. studying *The Racketeer's Glossary.*

Blackie: Fall 2019 supplement? There's changes.

Brickbat: Ah, crap.

Sound of police sirens drawing near. Screech of tires. The men all stand.

Crullah: It's the tran—I mean, choo-choo bulls! I didn't lose 'em after all!

Blackie: Fuck! Everyone am-scray!

Crullah: Huh?

The others hesitate as Crullah stands stock still.

Blackie: "Am-scray," "am-scray!" It's pig Latin!

Brickbat: It means "scram," as in "leave quickly!"

Crullah: Shit! That must've been in the Errata!

Instantly, the four hoodlums are swarmed by transit police officers. As they're led away, the grizzled POLICE CHIEF FINNEGAN draws Crullah aside.

Finnegan: Grade-A stoolery, me lad. Now Ma Choo Choo can wipe your slate clean.

Blackie (*as he's stuffed into a squad car*): Hey, bull! *He's* the fare-jumper, how come we're getting the collar? We're just a group of local businessmen having a pow-wow in cryptic terms in a public park on a cold day!

Finnegan: Tell it to the judge, Blackie. Tell it to the judge.

Blackie: You mean my nephew? I will.

Fade to black.   B

············ ◆ ············

Patrick L. Kennedy *is a regular contributor to this magazine.* **Paul R. Kennedy** *is a lawyer south of Boston whose sideburns got him a gig as an extra in* **Black Mass.** *Prior to this article, the brothers' main claim to fame was a music video, "We're All Wicked Liquored Up at the Upscale Downtown Irish Pub."*

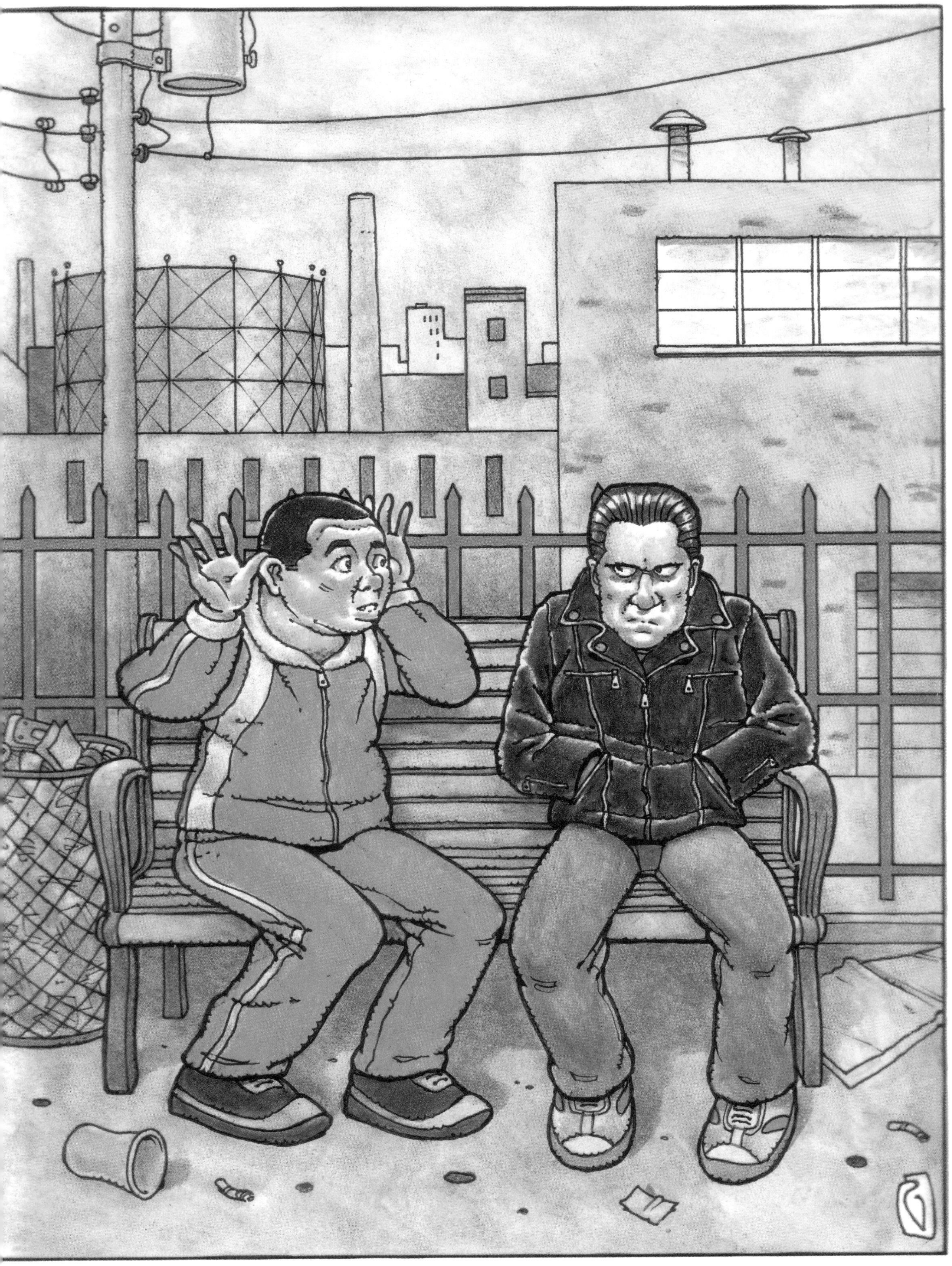

THE CHUCK-O-RAMA SUTRA

JAMES FINN GARNER & RICH SPARKS

Fig. 2:
The Turkey Shoot

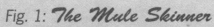

Fig. 1: *The Mule Skinner*

Fig. 3:
The OK Corral

FOR CONSENSUAL USE ONLY

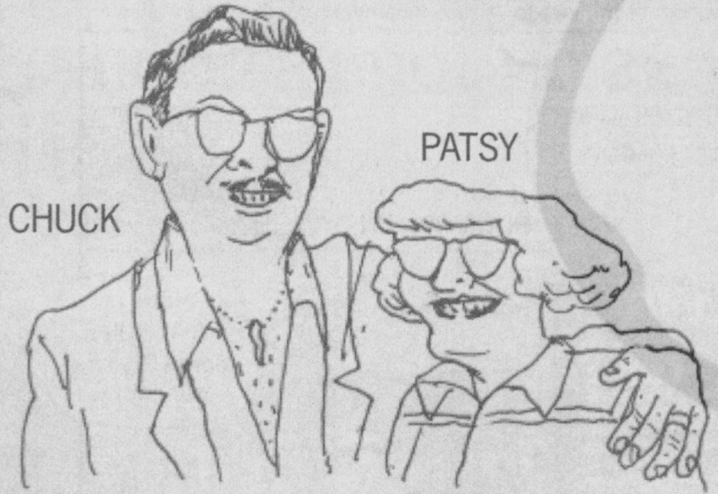
CHUCK
PATSY

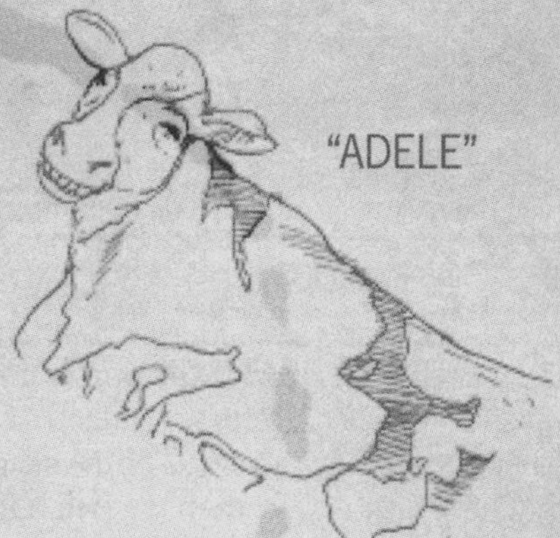
"ADELE"

Howdy, Friends!
Welcome to the Chuck-O-Rama Buffet!

For over 50 years, our family has been satisfying hungry travelers on Route 8 because we have only one rule: *People-pleasin'!* Whatever your appetite—for food, love, life!—people-pleasin' feeds 'em all! It also brings you a happy marriage, a healthy complexion, and the most popular buffet in mountain country. **Take this placemat with you**. If everyone got busy People-Pleasin', the *whole world would be a buffet!*

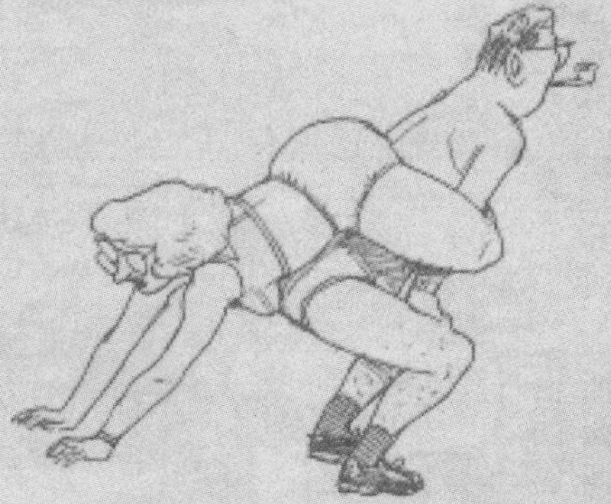

Fig. 4: ***The Prairie Fire***

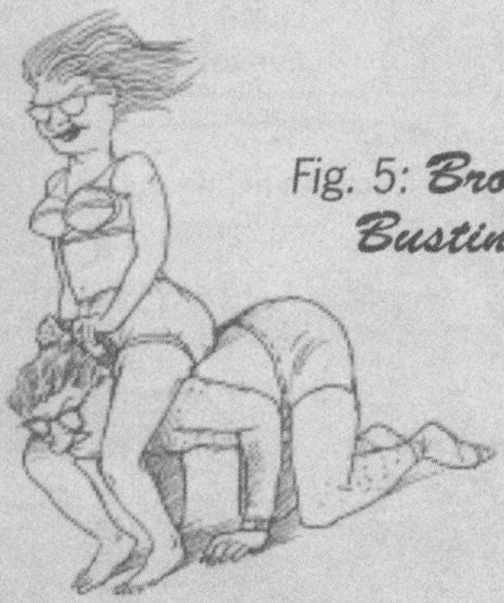

Fig. 5: ***Bronco Bustin'***

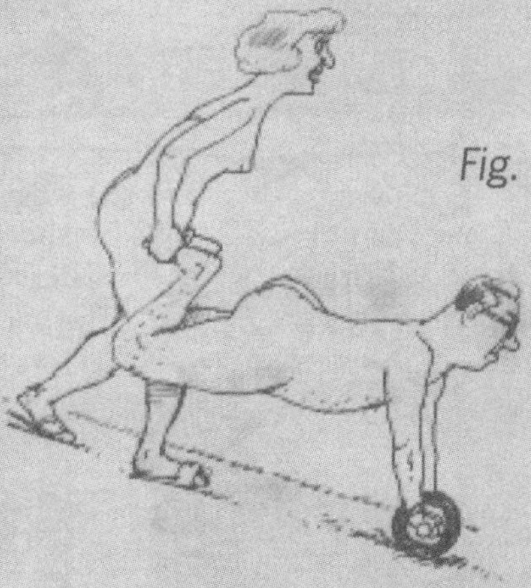

Fig. 6: ***Breakin' the Mustang***

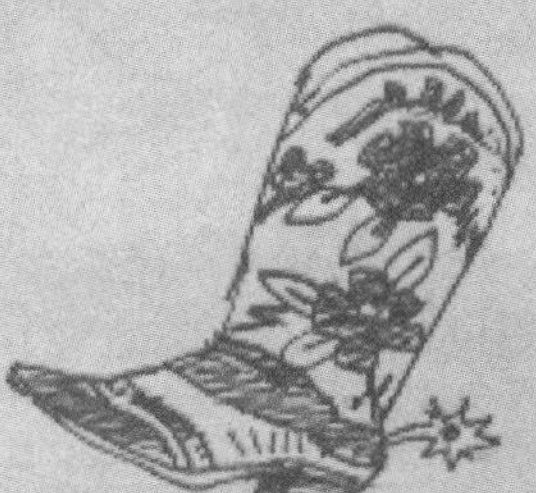

COURTESY OF

Chuck-o-Rama Buffet

5800 Red Arrow Highway • Wikieup, AZ 85360

JOHN WILCOCK: NEW YORK YEARS

A history of the formation of the 1960s Underground Press, from the co-founder of The Village Voice & the Underground Press Syndicate

HUNTER THOMPSON KNOCKS ON JOHN'S DOOR

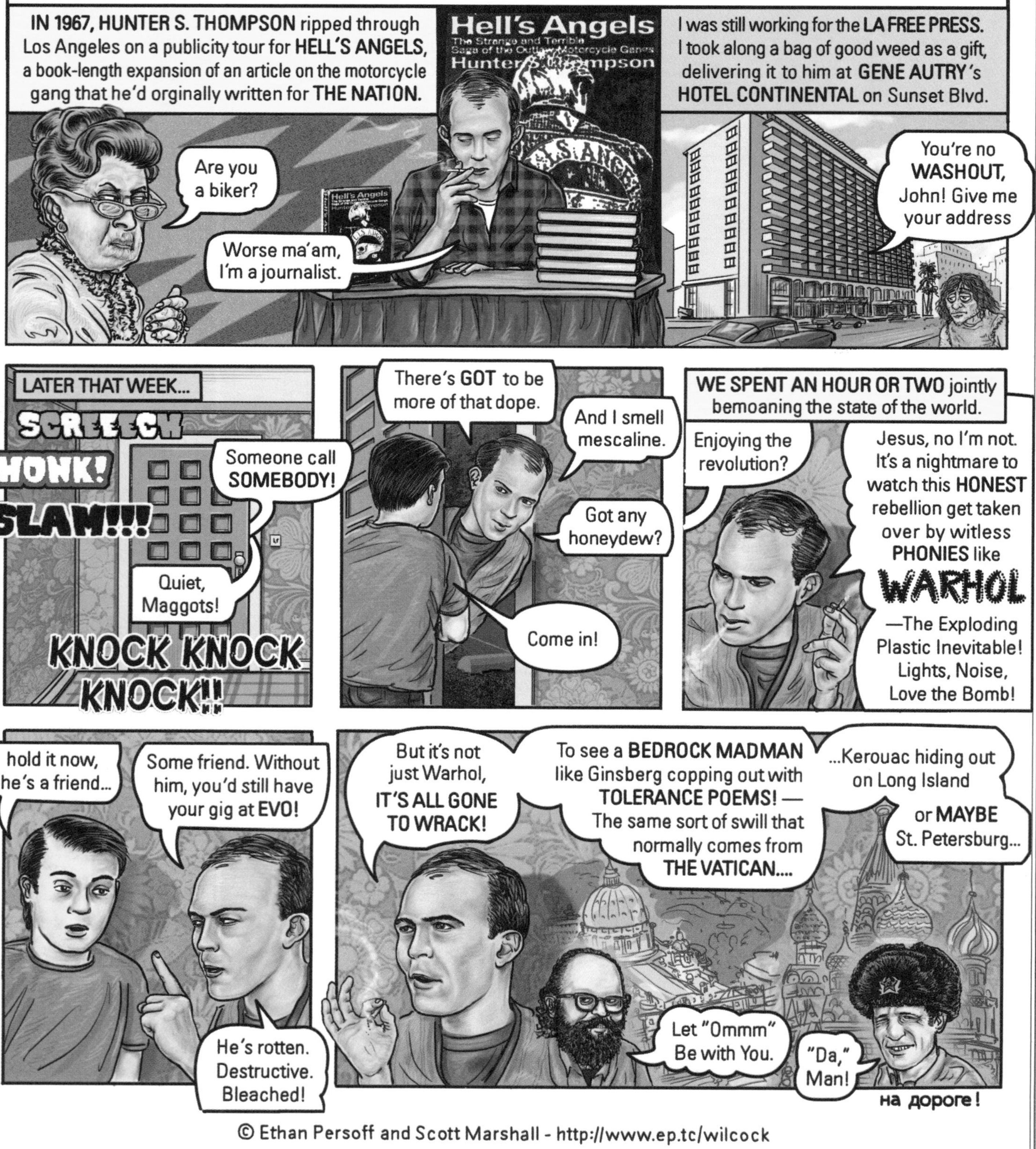
IN 1967, HUNTER S. THOMPSON ripped through Los Angeles on a publicity tour for HELL'S ANGELS, a book-length expansion of an article on the motorcycle gang that he'd orginally written for THE NATION.
Hell's Angels
Hunter S. Thompson
Are you a biker?
Worse ma'am, I'm a journalist.
I was still working for the LA FREE PRESS. I took along a bag of good weed as a gift, delivering it to him at GENE AUTRY's HOTEL CONTINENTAL on Sunset Blvd.
You're no WASHOUT, John! Give me your address
LATER THAT WEEK...
SCREEECH
HONK!
SLAM!!!
Someone call SOMEBODY!
Quiet, Maggots!
KNOCK KNOCK KNOCK!!
There's GOT to be more of that dope.
And I smell mescaline.
Got any honeydew?
Come in!
WE SPENT AN HOUR OR TWO jointly bemoaning the state of the world.
Enjoying the revolution?
Jesus, no I'm not. It's a nightmare to watch this HONEST rebellion get taken over by witless PHONIES like WARHOL —The Exploding Plastic Inevitable! Lights, Noise, Love the Bomb!
hold it now, he's a friend...
Some friend. Without him, you'd still have your gig at EVO!
He's rotten. Destructive. Bleached!
But it's not just Warhol, IT'S ALL GONE TO WRACK!
To see a BEDROCK MADMAN like Ginsberg copping out with TOLERANCE POEMS! — The same sort of swill that normally comes from THE VATICAN....
...Kerouac hiding out on Long Island
or MAYBE St. Petersburg...
Let "Ommm" Be with You.
"Da," Man!
на дороге!

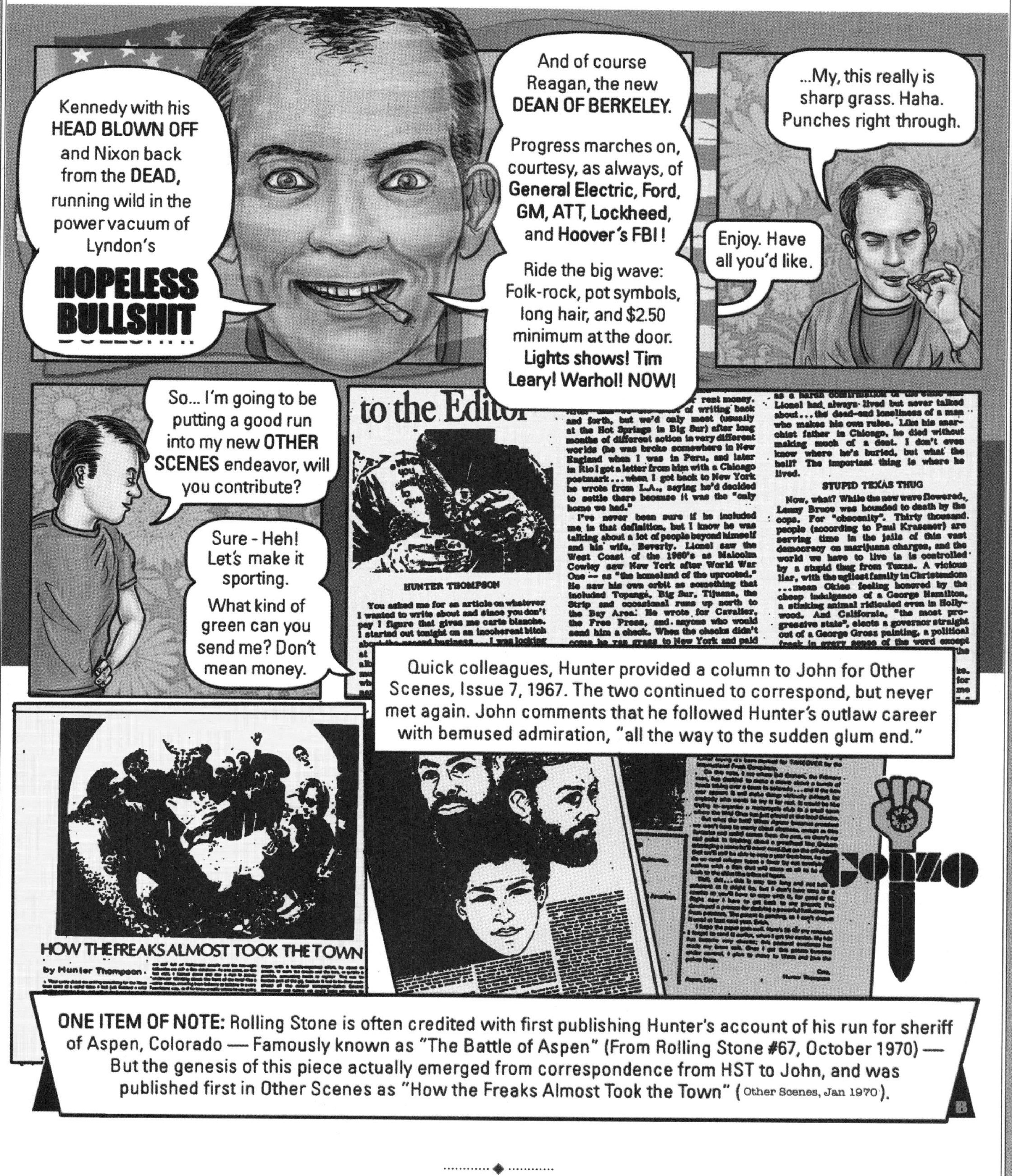
Kennedy with his HEAD BLOWN OFF and Nixon back from the DEAD, running wild in the power vacuum of Lyndon's HOPELESS BULLSHIT
And of course Reagan, the new DEAN OF BERKELEY.
Progress marches on, courtesy, as always, of General Electric, Ford, GM, ATT, Lockheed, and Hoover's FBI!
Ride the big wave: Folk-rock, pot symbols, long hair, and $2.50 minimum at the door. Lights shows! Tim Leary! Warhol! NOW!
...My, this really is sharp grass. Haha. Punches right through.
Enjoy. Have all you'd like.
So... I'm going to be putting a good run into my new OTHER SCENES endeavor, will you contribute?
Sure - Heh! Let's make it sporting.
What kind of green can you send me? Don't mean money.
to the Editor
HUNTER THOMPSON
STUPID TEXAS THUG
Quick colleagues, Hunter provided a column to John for Other Scenes, Issue 7, 1967. The two continued to correspond, but never met again. John comments that he followed Hunter's outlaw career with bemused admiration, "all the way to the sudden glum end."
HOW THE FREAKS ALMOST TOOK THE TOWN
by Hunter Thompson
GONZO
ONE ITEM OF NOTE: Rolling Stone is often credited with first publishing Hunter's account of his run for sheriff of Aspen, Colorado — Famously known as "The Battle of Aspen" (From Rolling Stone #67, October 1970) — But the genesis of this piece actually emerged from correspondence from HST to John, and was published first in Other Scenes as "How the Freaks Almost Took the Town" (Other Scenes, Jan 1970).

.... ◆ ....

Ethan Persoff *is an Austin-based sound designer, writer and cartoonist. His latest project is* **Spoken Word with Electronics***; learn more at http://www.ep.tc/.*

Scott Marshall *is an illustrator and painter in NYC and the greater Hudson Valley.*

FROM THE CAMPAIGN TRAIL OR THEREABOUTS

A New Satire Novel by Michael Bleicher & Andy Newton

"I almost died laughing. In fact, I probably should be dead."
—Richard Lewis (Recovering comedian)

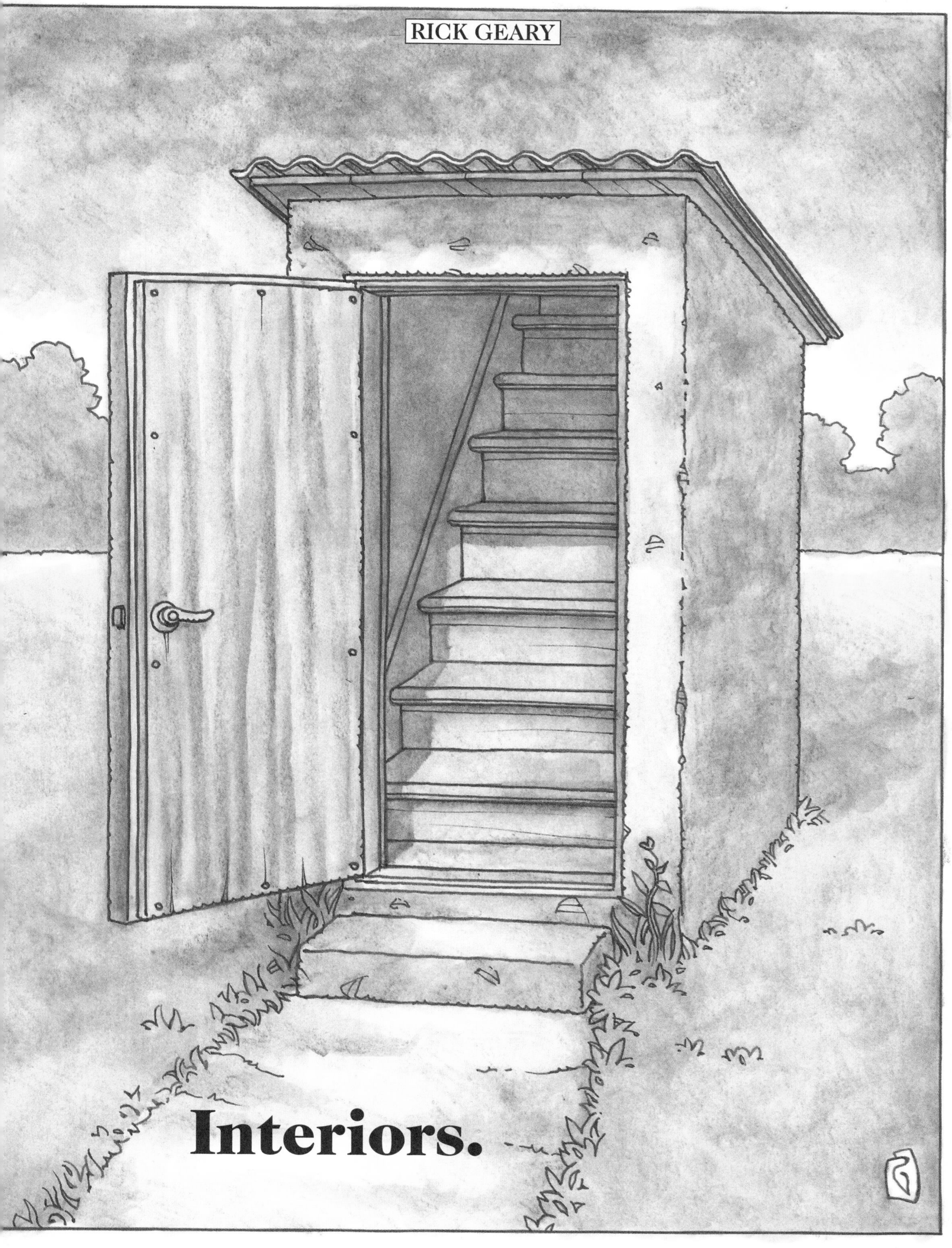
RICK GEARY
Interiors.

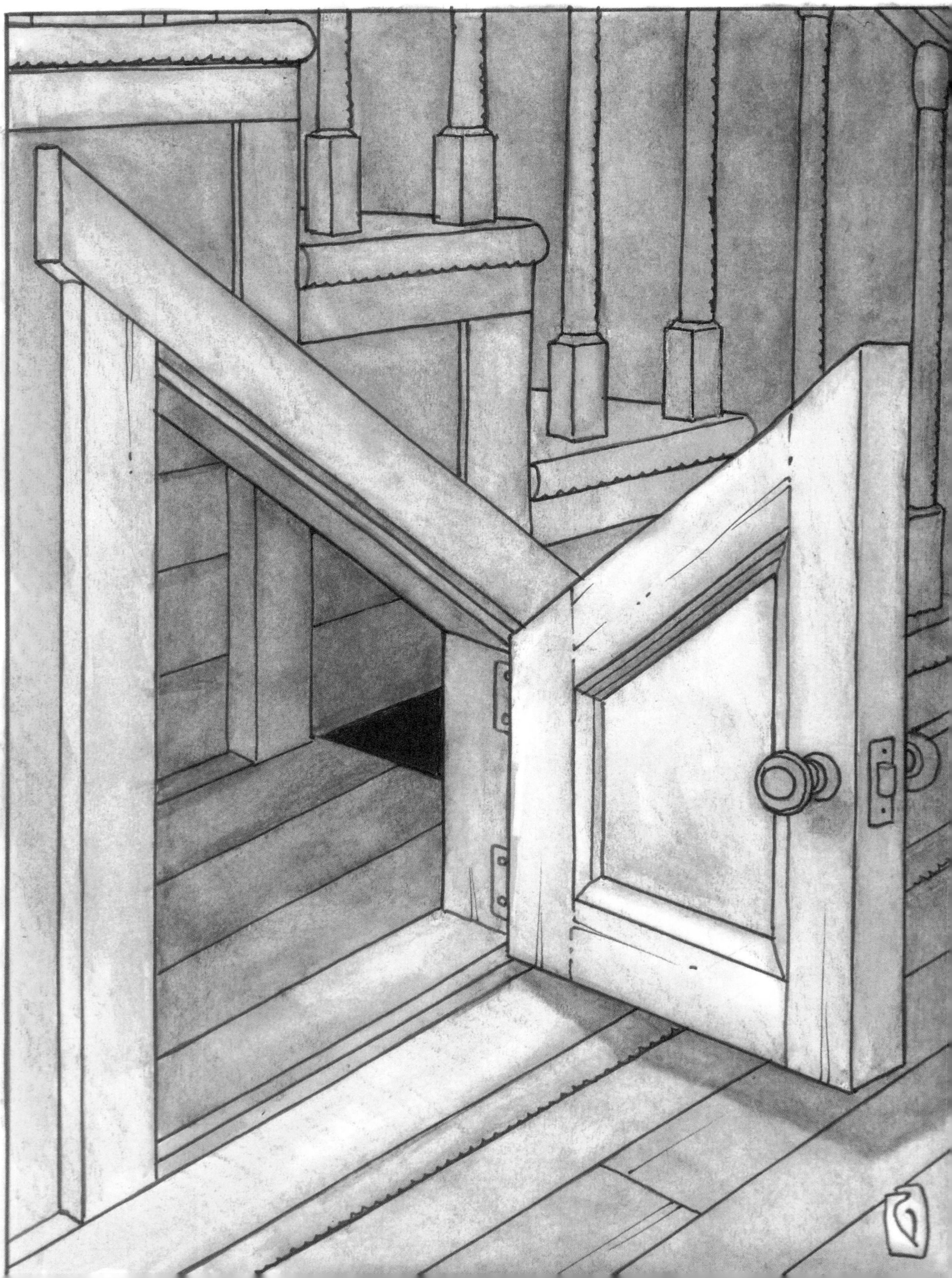

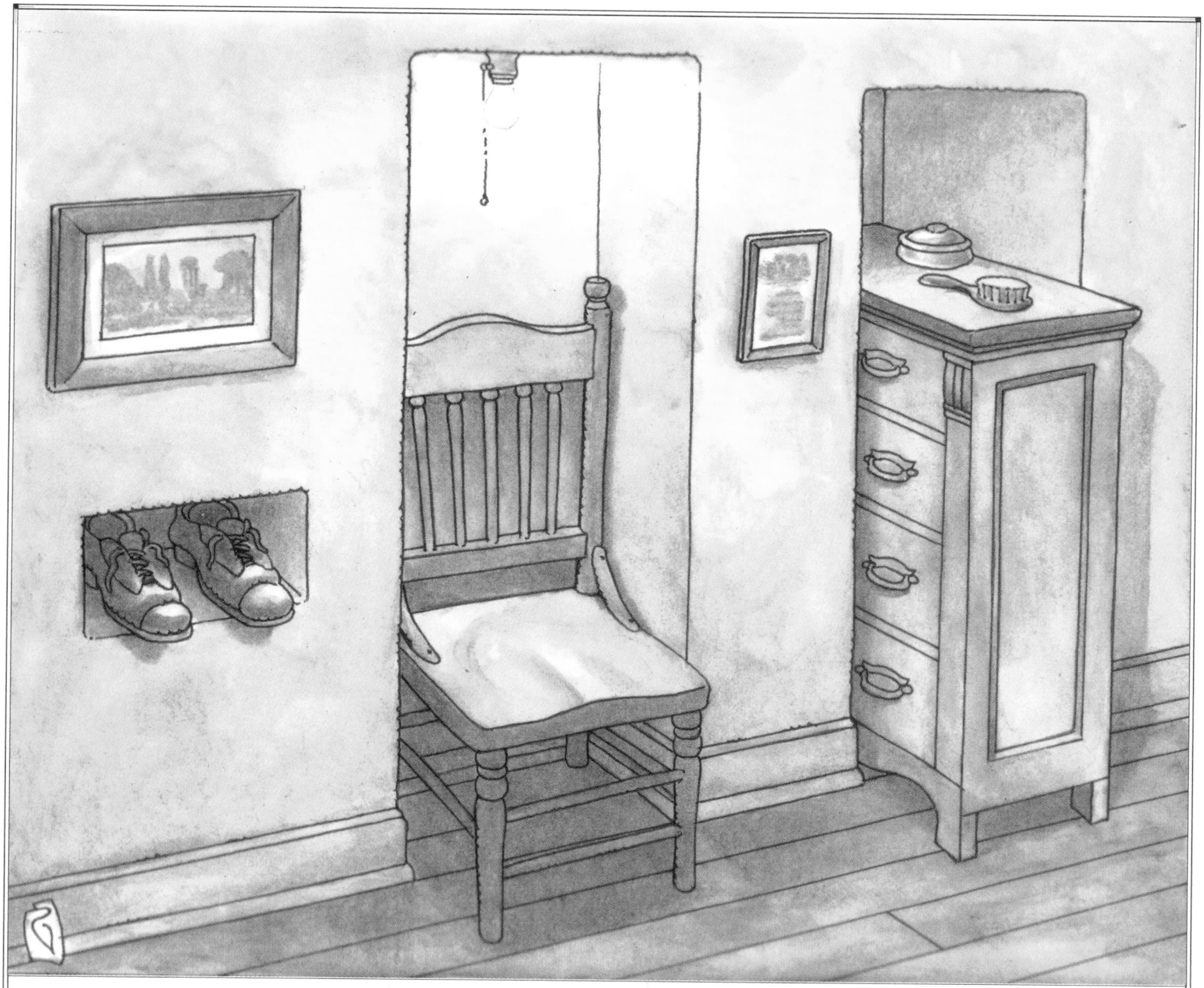

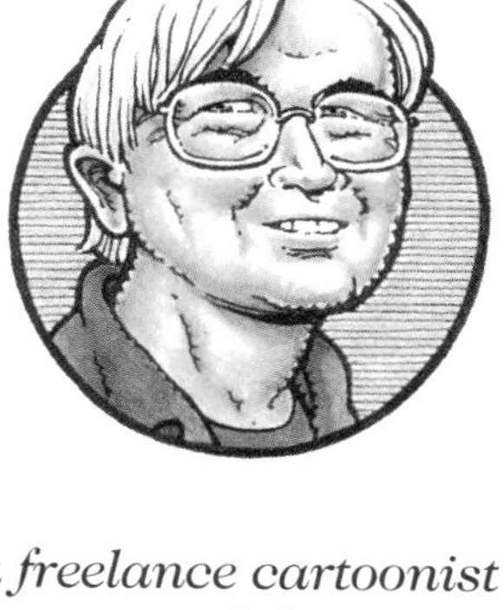

Rick Geary *has been a freelance cartoonist and illustrator for 45 years but only recently has started doing these strange interiors. He lives in Carrizozo, New Mexico.*

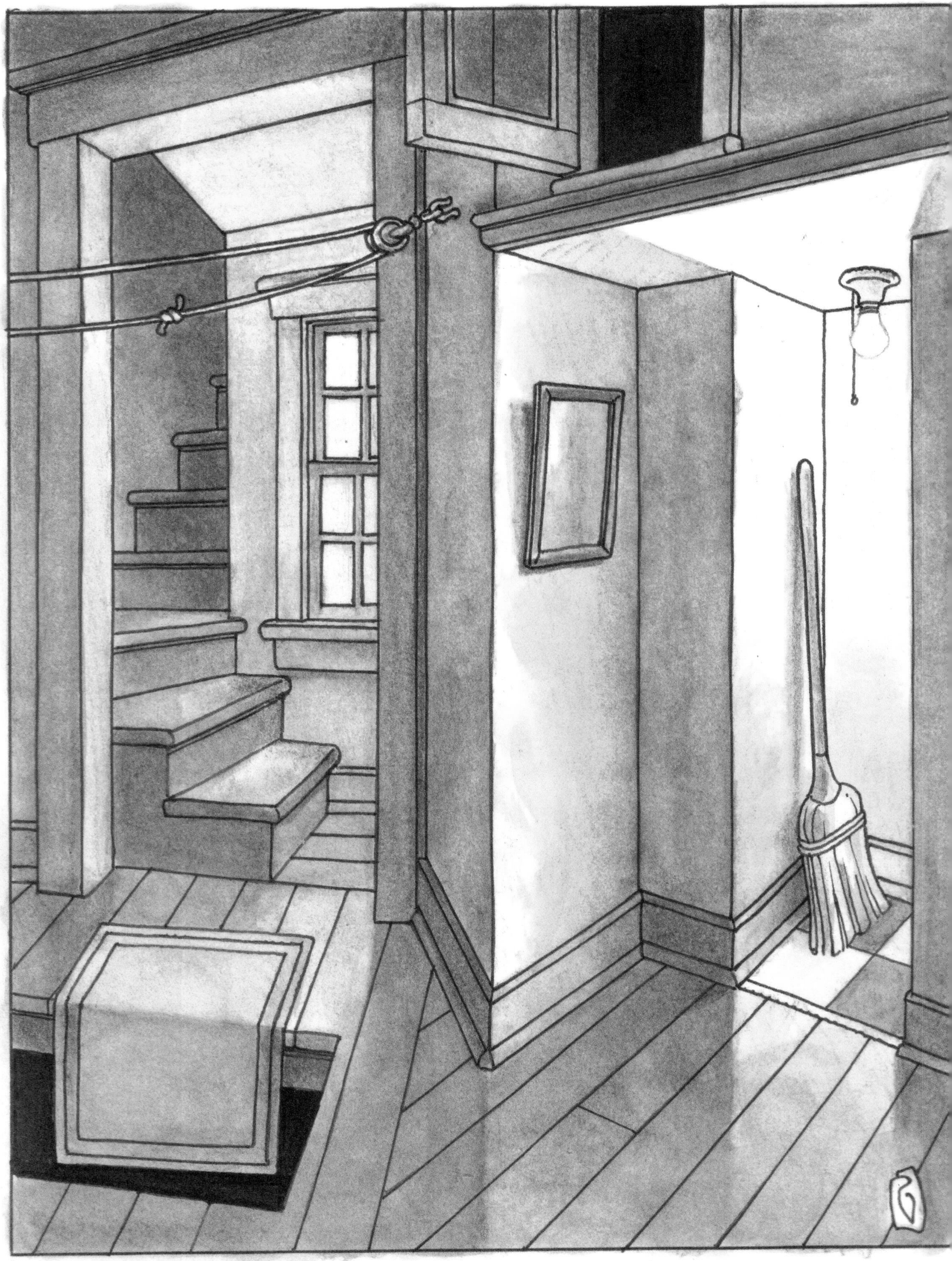

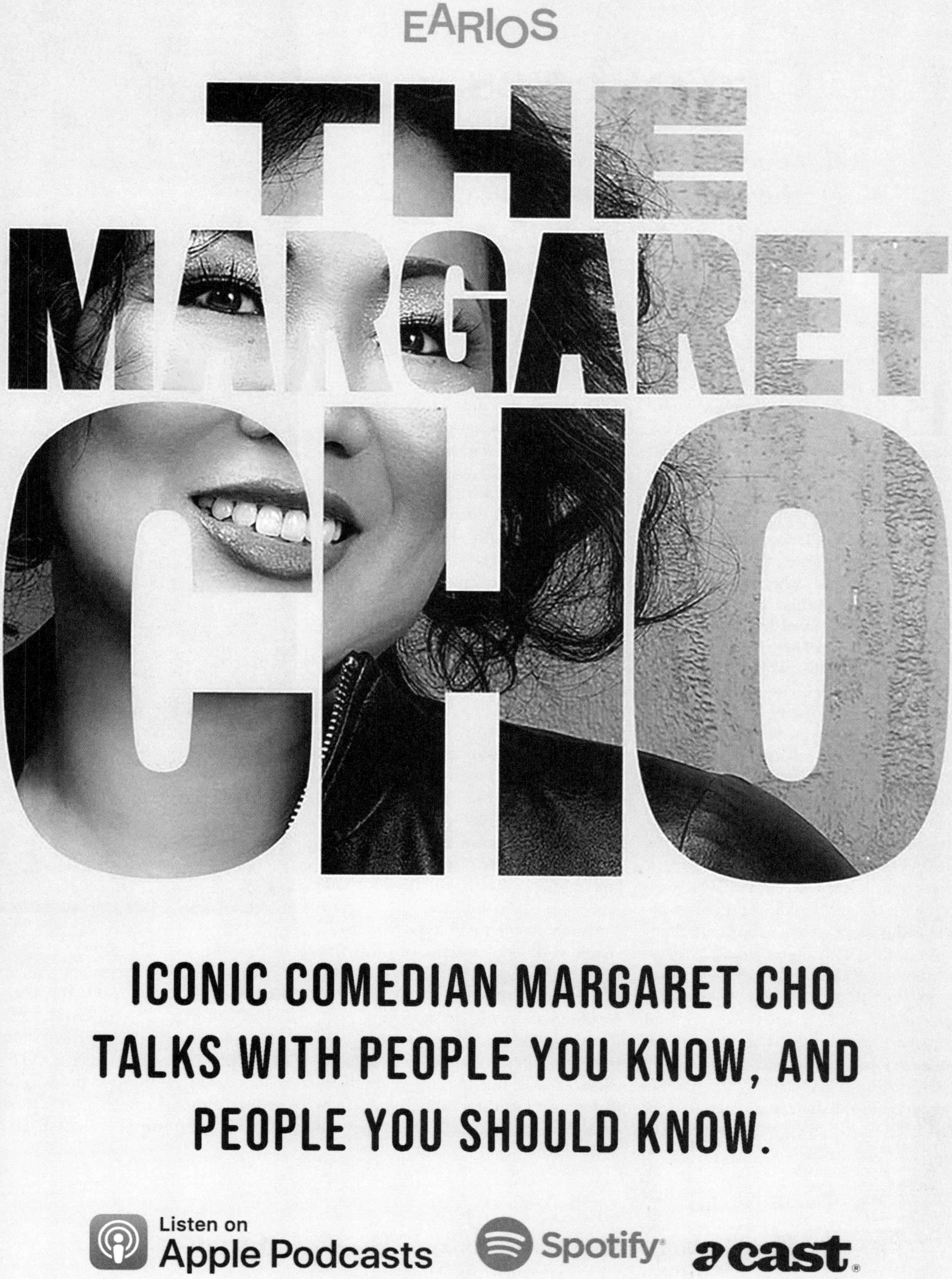
EARIOS
THE MARGARET CHO
ICONIC COMEDIAN MARGARET CHO TALKS WITH PEOPLE YOU KNOW, AND PEOPLE YOU SHOULD KNOW.
Listen on Apple Podcasts
Spotify
acast

Crazy Eyes

Whenever we think someone else might be looking at us…crazy eyes rears its ugly head.

Body dysmorphia has got to go. This is this ignant disease where you don't know what you look like. It's similar to another condition that I believe is called "crazy eyes"— not the way that other people see you ("Look at that fool Marty Feldman— he's got some crazy eyes!"), but the way you see yourself. The insanity, which we use as our vision, surfaces when we get dressed to go somewhere where we think people will be looking at us with the same crazy eyes that we have. There is a cure for this disease, but, sadly, people don't really think that it works. The cure is, nobody cares what you look like except you and your crazy eyes. It's a tough pill to swallow, like a horse pill you have to take with a gallon of Sparklett's to get the whole thing down, and even then it just sticks in your throat, creating a pharmaceutical Adam's apple. That's nasty, thinking that nobody cares what you look like except you, but that's because they're too busy looking at themselves, thinking about what's wrong with them and dealing with their own crazy eyes. And even if they do care about what you look like, it's only a momentary, fleeting thought, a brief overview and comparison between what you look like against what they think they look like, so the thought isn't really about you, it's about them and their crazy eyes, not you and your crazy eyes. So fuck it. You're both crazy, and that's final.

Crazy eyes is not fatal, but it can lead to other diseases that are. It is a gateway to other diseases, just like marijuana is a gateway to other drugs, and the "munchies," which is a gateway to crazy eyes. If left untreated, crazy eyes will get worse, and could develop into disordered eating, which leads to the wonderful world of Bulimarama (Try 'em all! Bulimarexia, Good Ol' Binge'n'Purge, Exercise Bulimia, Laxative Bulimia, "I'm starting my diet tomorrow so I have to get it all in before midnight" Bulimia, Honey Mustard Bulimia) and the Grim Reaper, Anorexia, coming to claim the lives of young women, much like consumption did in the Victorian era. She's a tall, gaunt figure, chic and wiry, draped in black muslin, but instead of a scythe this skeleton has a fork and spoon, because even death thinks you need a good hearty meal of macaroni and cheese to fortify you for your long journey into the afterlife.

And then, what if you die before you reach your goal weight of forty-five pounds? Perhaps your narrow-ass ghost will be condemned to roam the metropolitan shopping malls of your past, like the poor old prisoners who, even in death, refuse to leave their cells on Alcatraz. Will the dressing-room doors in Urban Outfitters creak open, then slam shut, for no reason? Supernatural shrieks coming from inside the slatted stalls, "I NEED A LARGER SIZE!!!!!!!! AHHHHHHHHHHH!!!!!!! HELPPPPPP MEEEEEEEE!" as clerks rush in and find nobody there, nothing but the lingering scent of almond vomit, a chill in the air and a size 0 pair of Frankie B. jeans

---

◆

Beloved comedian and recovering Crazy Eyes sufferer **Margaret Cho** *lives in Los Angeles.*

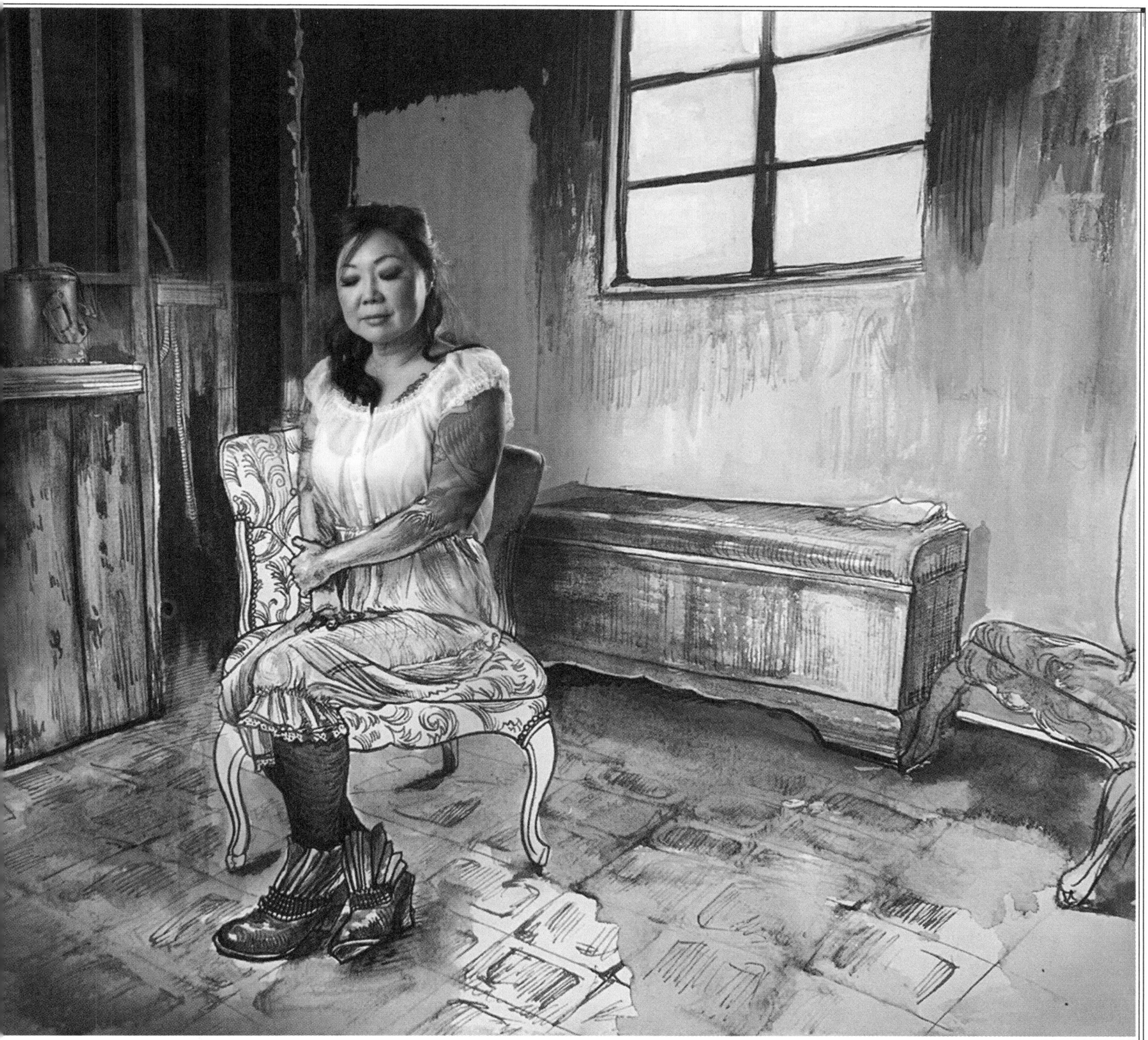

Margaret Cho, photographed in Los Angeles in January 2020. Photo by **B.A. VAN SISE** & **MICHELLE J. LI**.

turned inside-out on the floor.

Or maybe you will find your way to heaven. God knows, you deserve it, having put yourself through a correspondence course in Hell, getting your GED in suffering in the precious few days of your tragic life, all the while maintaining a rigorous workout schedule and an insufficient caloric intake. Will the first thing you ask when you reach the Pearly Gates, which, thankfully for you, is atop an impossibly long flight of cement steps, be, "Where's the gym?"

Crazy eyes is wildly contagious. Everybody has some form of it. The people who pick and choose the images that we see daily on TV, in movies, in magazines and advertising—everywhere—have the craziest eyes of all, which is why this malady is worse than most other forms of biological warfare. Smallpox's got nothing on CE. Crazy eyes is the ultimate weapon of mass destruction because it works slowly, eroding the mind and the spirit and eventually the body, pound by pound, inch by inch, and it sets its crazy sights upon young women, who provide the gateway to future generations. If crazy eyes escalated to pandemic proportions, which is the next level up from the epidemic we have now, there would be a massive shortage of females capable of reproduction. Even if all of us didn't die right away from CE, and the diseases caused by CE infection, low body weight would make menstruation impossible, and procreation rare and difficult. This, along with the few remaining fertile women unwilling to

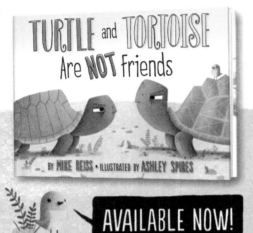

become pregnant because they don't want to look "fat," would eventually kill off the human race altogether.

And today, with the advent of the Internet, and the crazy eyes of the media enforcing their crazy vision on the global optic nerve, as the world gets smaller through technology, becomes more and more uniform in its tastes, customs, practices, beliefs, ideals, collective dreams and nightmares—as cultures homogenize and pasteurize and become one solid block of cheese nobody is going to eat—crazy eyes will spread faster than a wildfire in Granada Hills. Don't act like I'm some crackpot who is about to put this manifesto on a sandwich board and walk up and down the Third Street Promenade with a megaphone and those joke glasses with the eyeballs on springs popping out. You know crazy eyes is real. You have probably suffered from it at some time in your life. I'm a CE survivor, and I live in fear for others who may not have the strength or even the reason to save themselves.

There is hope. Crazy eyes is even easier to fix than astigmatism or glaucoma. You don't even need to get laser surgery on your retinas. Prevention is the best line of defense. When you look at yourself in the mirror, you can say only one thing: "I look fine." Do not think about what you ate today or yesterday—or ever. Do not change your outfit. Do not say anything about yourself to yourself. Do not think about the way you look again. Think instead about how nice it is that somebody loves you, or that your dog is so sweet when she follows the sunlight as it moves across the sky, napping at every window with such regularity that you could set your watch by her gentle snores and dog dreams, or that you miss someone and maybe you should call them, or if you can't call them because they are not around anymore think about how much you loved them and why, or how much you hated them and why, or about how the thoughts of love or hate can be equally provocative and tantalizing, or that sometimes there really is an easy way to do things, or that popcorn is always a good thing to get at the movies, or that you can stay home and watch TV if you want to, not even committing to a specific show— just flipping for no reason except that you want to, or that it's weird that certain colors are called that, like why is blue called blue—or whatever ignant or smart or sad or stupid or funny or brilliant or ridiculous thought to fill your mind with instead of "Do I look okay?"

Stop crazy eyes before it starts. You look fine.

B

"You're just making up that last part."

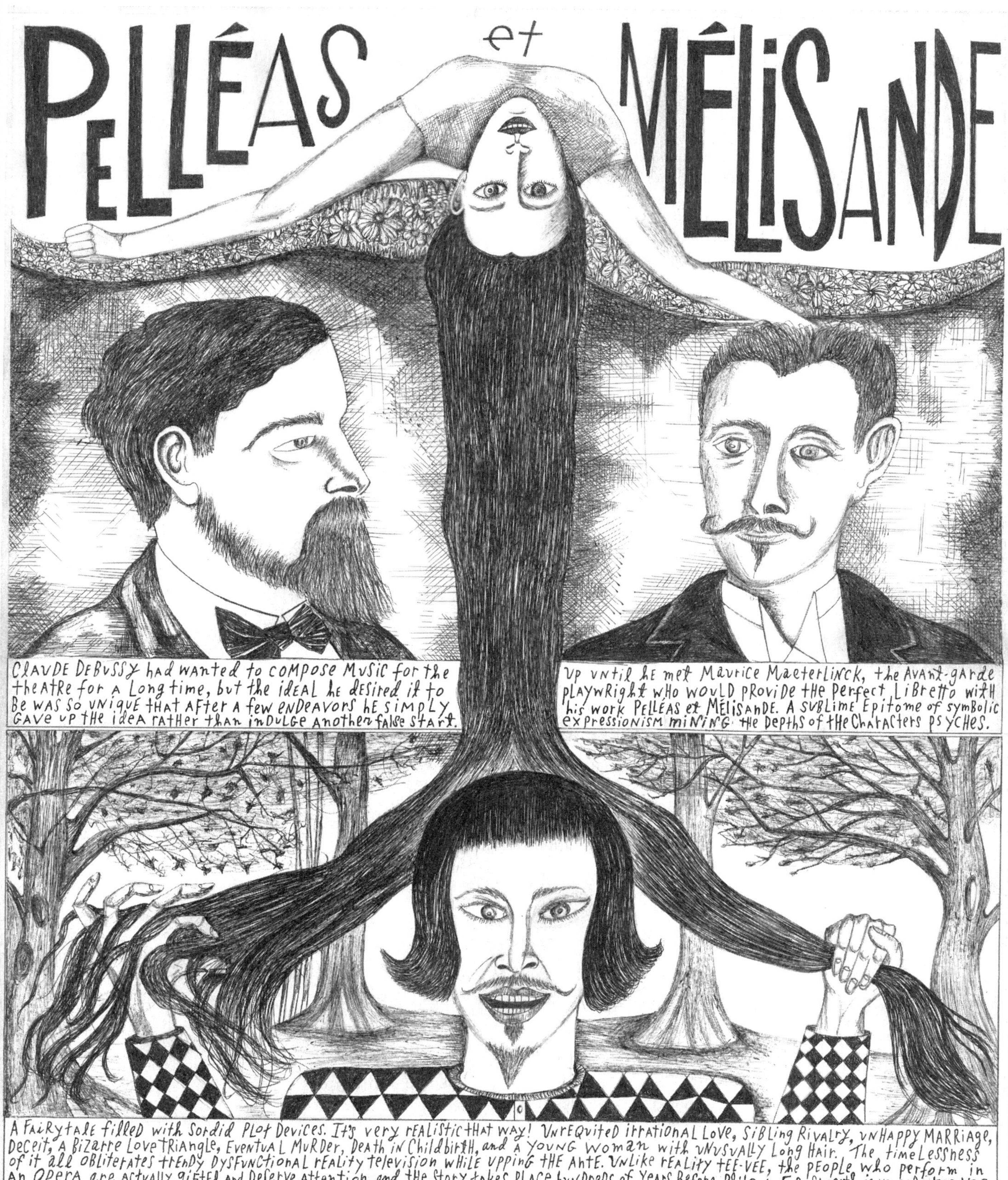
PELLÉAS et MÉLISANDE
CLAUDE DEBUSSY had wanted to compose music for the theatre for a long time, but the ideal he desired it to be was so unique that after a few endeavors he simply gave up the idea rather than indulge another false start.
Up until he met Maurice Maeterlinck, the avant-garde playwright who would provide the perfect libretto with his work PELLÉAS et MÉLISANDE. A sublime epitome of symbolic expressionism mining the depths of the characters psyches.
A fairytale filled with sordid plot devices. It's very realistic that way! Unrequited irrational love, sibling rivalry, unhappy marriage, deceit, a bizarre love triangle, eventual murder, death in childbirth, and a young woman with unusually long hair. The timelessness of it all obliterates trendy dysfunctional reality television while upping the ante. Unlike reality tee-vee, the people who perform in an opera are actually gifted and deserve attention, and the story takes place hundreds of years before Philo T. Farnsworth invented tee-vee.

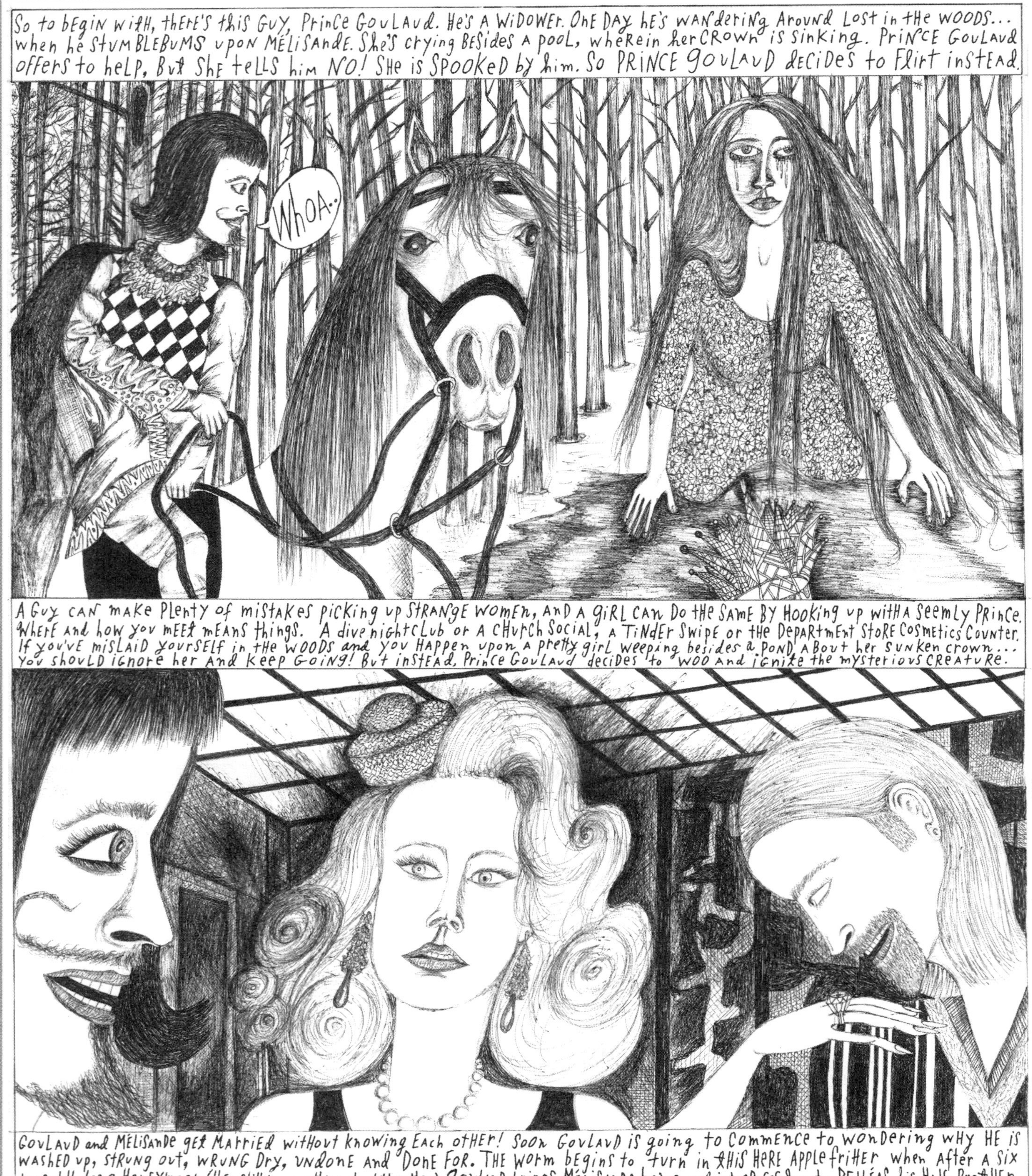
So to begin with, there's this guy, Prince Goulaud. He's a widower. One day he's wandering around lost in the woods... when he stumblebums upon Mélisande. She's crying besides a pool, wherein her crown is sinking. Prince Goulaud offers to help, but she tells him NO! She is spooked by him. So Prince Goulaud decides to flirt instead.
Whoa..
A guy can make plenty of mistakes picking up strange women, and a girl can do the same by hooking up with a seemly prince. Where and how you meet means things. A dive nightclub or a church social, a Tinder swipe or the department store cosmetics counter. If you've mislaid yourself in the woods and you happen upon a pretty girl weeping besides a pond about her sunken crown... You should ignore her and keep going! But instead, Prince Goulaud decides to woo and ignite the mysterious creature.
Goulaud and Mélisande get married without knowing each other! Soon Goulaud is going to commence to wondering why he is washed up, strung out, wrung dry, undone and done for. The worm begins to turn in this here apple fritter when after a six month long honeymoon (they still know nothing about the other) Goulaud brings Mélisande home and introduces her to Pelléas his half-brother.

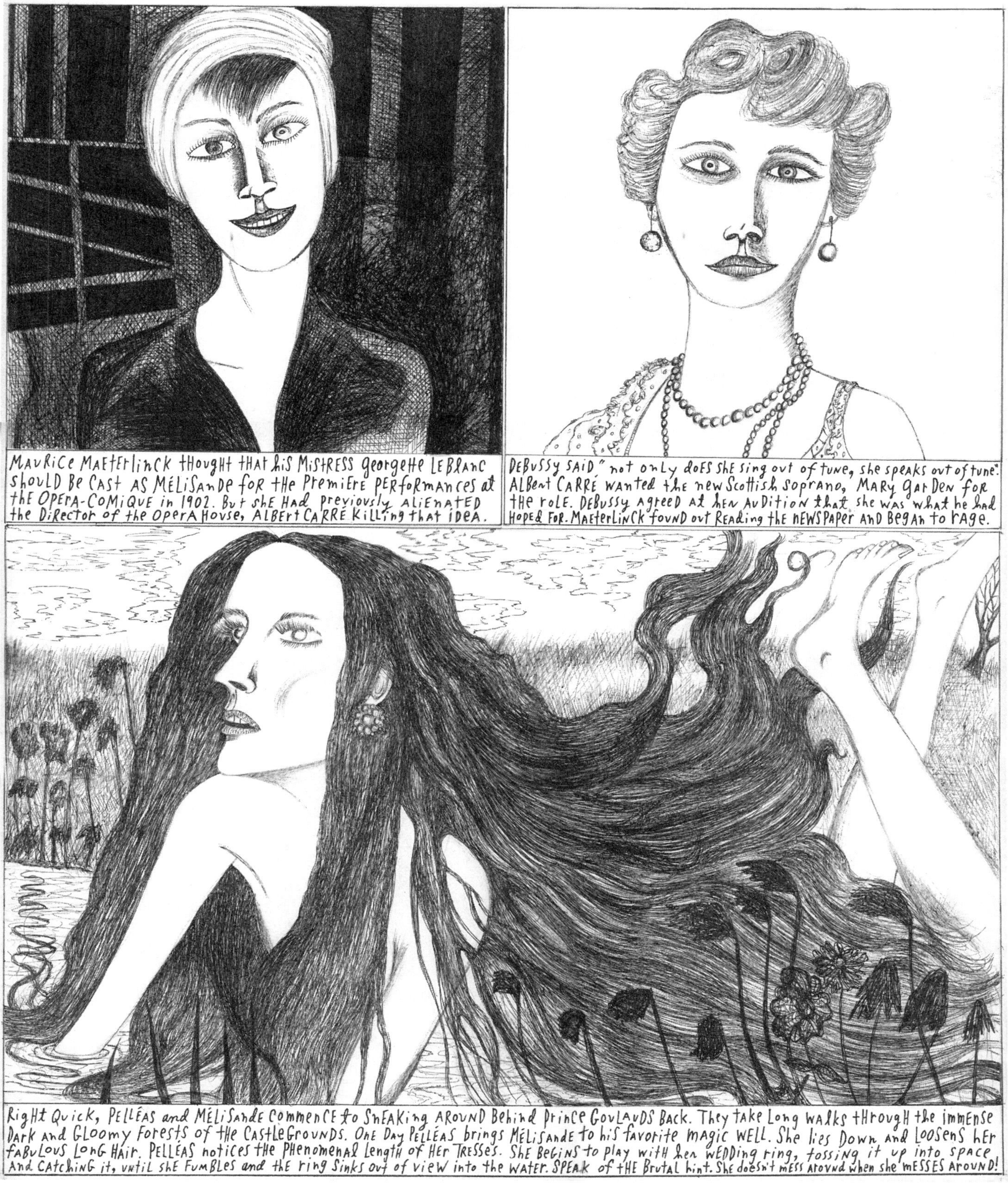
MAURICE MAETERLINCK THOUGHT THAT HIS MISTRESS GEORGETTE LEBLANC SHOULD BE CAST AS MÉLISANDE FOR THE PREMIERE PERFORMANCES AT THE OPERA-COMIQUE IN 1902. BUT SHE HAD PREVIOUSLY ALIENATED THE DIRECTOR OF THE OPERA HOUSE, ALBERT CARRÉ KILLING THAT IDEA.
DEBUSSY SAID "NOT ONLY DOES SHE SING OUT OF TUNE, SHE SPEAKS OUT OF TUNE". ALBERT CARRÉ WANTED THE NEW SCOTTISH SOPRANO, MARY GARDEN FOR THE ROLE. DEBUSSY AGREED AT HER AUDITION THAT SHE WAS WHAT HE HAD HOPED FOR. MAETERLINCK FOUND OUT READING THE NEWSPAPER AND BEGAN TO RAGE.
RIGHT QUICK, PELLÉAS AND MÉLISANDE COMMENCE TO SNEAKING AROUND BEHIND PRINCE GOULAUD'S BACK. THEY TAKE LONG WALKS THROUGH THE IMMENSE DARK AND GLOOMY FORESTS OF THE CASTLE GROUNDS. ONE DAY PELLÉAS BRINGS MÉLISANDE TO HIS FAVORITE MAGIC WELL. SHE LIES DOWN AND LOOSENS HER FABULOUS LONG HAIR. PELLÉAS NOTICES THE PHENOMENAL LENGTH OF HER TRESSES. SHE BEGINS TO PLAY WITH HER WEDDING RING, TOSSING IT UP INTO SPACE AND CATCHING IT, UNTIL SHE FUMBLES AND THE RING SINKS OUT OF VIEW INTO THE WATER. SPEAK OF THE BRUTAL HINT. SHE DOESN'T MESS AROUND WHEN SHE MESSES AROUND!

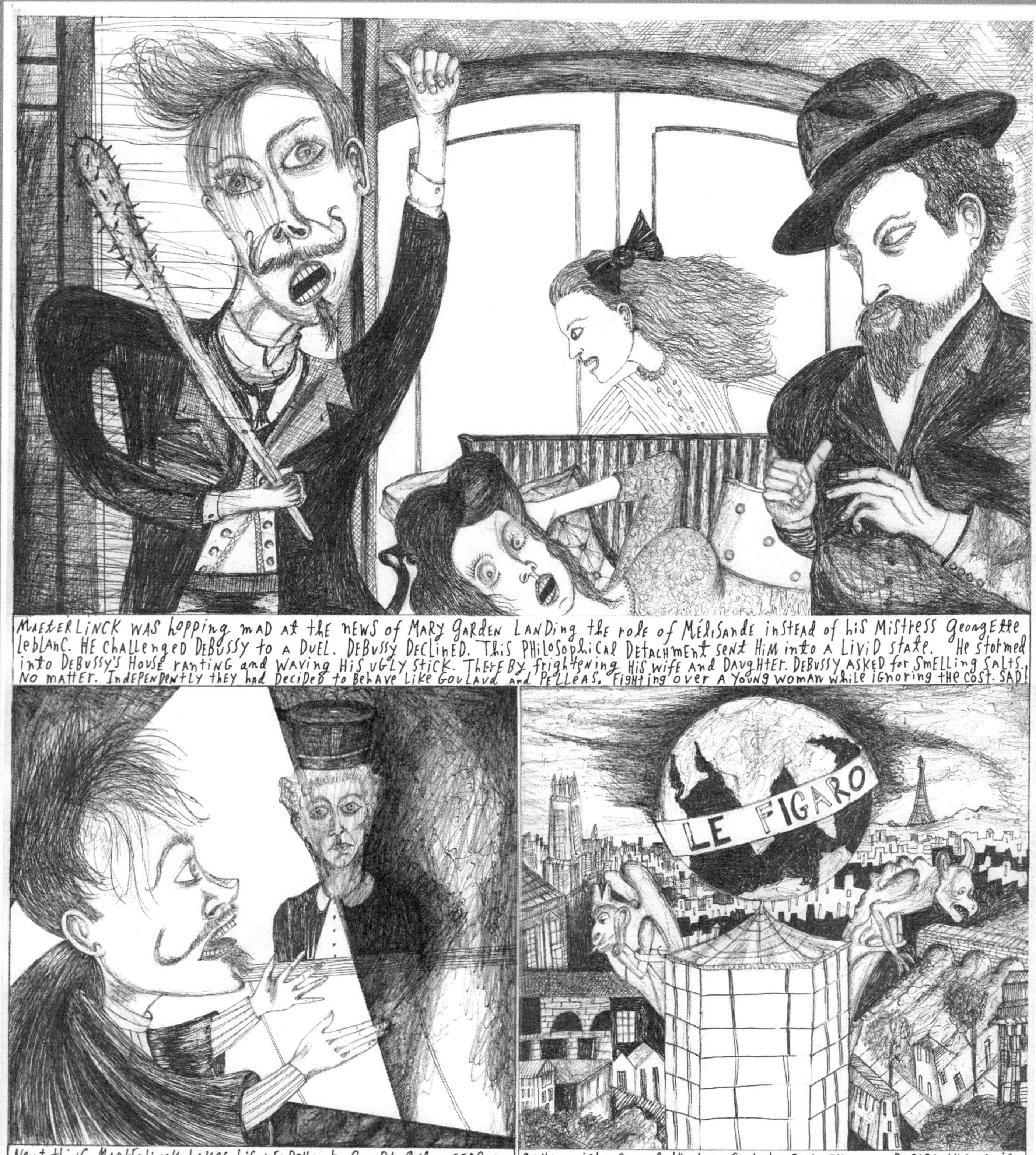
MAETERLINCK WAS hopping mAD At the NEWS of MARY GARDEN LANDing the role of MÉLiSANDE instead of his Mistress GeorGette LeBLANC. HE ChALLenged DEBUSSY to A DUEL. DEBUSSY DECLINED. This PHiLOSOPHiCAL DETACHMENT SENT HiM into A LIViD state. He stormed into DEBUSSY's HOUSE ranting and WAVING HIS UGLY STICK. THEREBY frightening HiS wife AND DAUGHTER. DEBUSSY ASKED for SMELLING SALTS. NO MATTER. INDEPENDENTLY they had DECIDED to BEHAVE LIKE GOULAUD and PELLEAS. Fighting over A YOUNG WOMAN while ignoring the cost. SAD!
LE FIGARO
Next thing MAETERLINCK takes his VENDETTA to COURT. Who NEEDS A Hitman, when you can hire an attorney? DEBUSSY thought this "Little short of PATHOLOGICAL". It BECAME TRANSPARENT to the Court that the issue WAS A feud so to speak and they decide to clear DEBUSSY's NAME.
WHEN VIOLENCE and the LAW fail to QUENCH your DESIRE, there is A LWAYS journalism. MAETERLINCK PENS an open Letter to LE FIGARO denouncing DEBUSSY and the OPERA and wanting it to FLOP, "prompt and resoundingly". Once AGAIN CLAUDE DEBUSSY ignores the insult.

Mélisande is singing by her window while combing her hair. Out for a dark stroll, Pelléas happens on by, encouraging her to spill her hair down to him. Engulfed, he proceeds to have his way with her wig.

At this point in the story, it ought to occur to just about anyone that this girls' hair wants cutting! Really now, all of this lust driving only towards tragedy would come to an abrupt end with a pixie cut! Somebody please write the barber of Seville into this libretto, or even Sweeney Todd if it has to come to that.

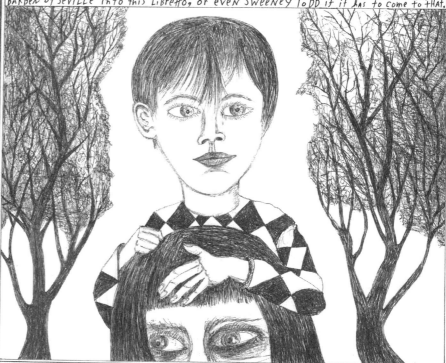

Just think of the money we could make, selling the wigs to Cher. Goulaud has been peepin' and a hidin' the entire time. He places his little son Yniold, from his first marriage onto his shoulders to spy into Mélisandes window as she and Pelléas tryst. Later that night, rageful and jealous, Goulaud throws her around by her hair . . .

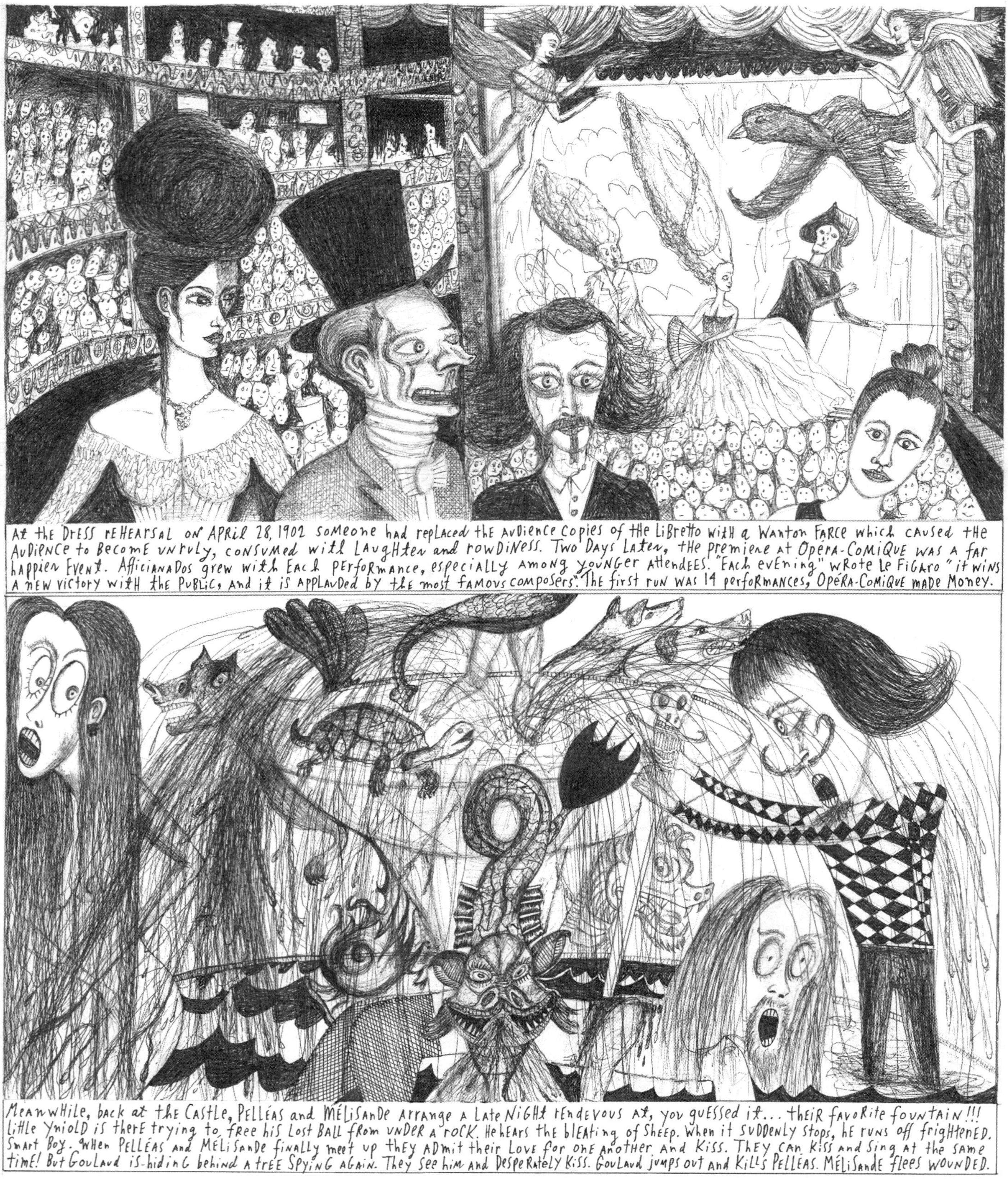
At the Dress rehearsal on April 28, 1902 someone had replaced the audience copies of the Libretto with a Wanton Farce which caused the audience to become unruly, consumed with laughter and rowdiness. Two days later, the premiere at Opéra-Comique was a far happier event. Afficianados grew with each performance, especially among younger attendees. "Each evening" wrote Le Figaro "it wins a new victory with the public, and it is applauded by the most famous composers". The first run was 14 performances, Opéra-Comique made money.
Meanwhile, back at the Castle, Pelléas and Mélisande arrange a late night rendevous at, you guessed it... their favorite fountain!!! Little Yniold is there trying to free his lost ball from under a rock. He hears the bleating of sheep. When it suddenly stops, he runs off frightened. Smart boy. When Pelléas and Mélisande finally meet up they admit their love for one another and kiss. They can kiss and sing at the same time! But Goulaud is hiding behind a tree spying again. They see him and desperately kiss. Goulaud jumps out and kills Pelléas. Mélisande flees wounded.

B

THESE COLORS WILL MAKE YOU FEEL HUNGRY

FIND A UNIQUE RESTAURANT EXPERIENCE
IN JOHN DONOHUE'S NEW BOOK

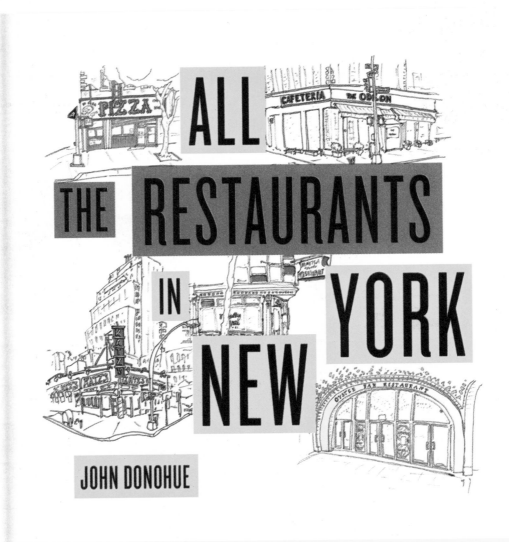

ALL THE RESTAURANTS IN NEW YORK

JOHN DONOHUE

"John Donohue is the Rembrandt of New York City's restaurant facades."
—**Adam Platt**, restaurant critic, *New York* magazine

"If you know someone who's wild for a special New York restaurant,
this is the perfect present."
-**Ruth Reichl**

Includes *that* Italian restaurant that brings in grandmothers from around the world to cook!

NOTES FROM A SMALL PLANET

...and wait'll you see their Ancestry.com results! • **By Rick Geary**

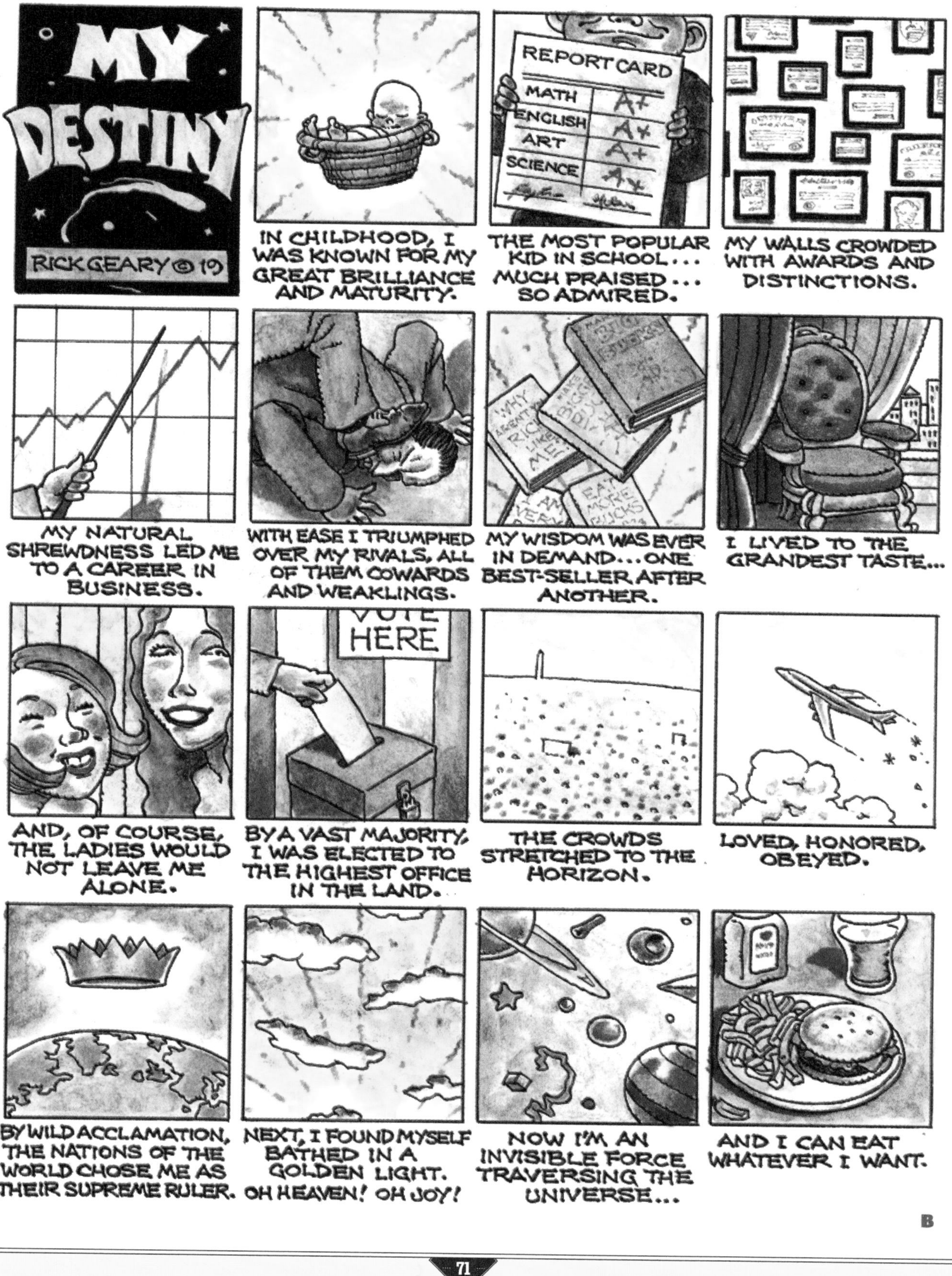
MY DESTINY
RICK GEARY © 19
IN CHILDHOOD, I WAS KNOWN FOR MY GREAT BRILLIANCE AND MATURITY.
REPORT CARD
MATH
ENGLISH
ART
SCIENCE
THE MOST POPULAR KID IN SCHOOL... MUCH PRAISED... SO ADMIRED.
MY WALLS CROWDED WITH AWARDS AND DISTINCTIONS.
MY NATURAL SHREWDNESS LED ME TO A CAREER IN BUSINESS.
WITH EASE I TRIUMPHED OVER MY RIVALS, ALL OF THEM COWARDS AND WEAKLINGS.
MY WISDOM WAS EVER IN DEMAND... ONE BEST-SELLER AFTER ANOTHER.
I LIVED TO THE GRANDEST TASTE...
AND, OF COURSE, THE LADIES WOULD NOT LEAVE ME ALONE.
VOTE HERE
BY A VAST MAJORITY, I WAS ELECTED TO THE HIGHEST OFFICE IN THE LAND.
THE CROWDS STRETCHED TO THE HORIZON.
LOVED, HONORED, OBEYED.
BY WILD ACCLAMATION, THE NATIONS OF THE WORLD CHOSE ME AS THEIR SUPREME RULER.
NEXT, I FOUND MYSELF BATHED IN A GOLDEN LIGHT. OH HEAVEN! OH JOY!
NOW I'M AN INVISIBLE FORCE TRAVERSING THE UNIVERSE...
AND I CAN EAT WHATEVER I WANT.

B

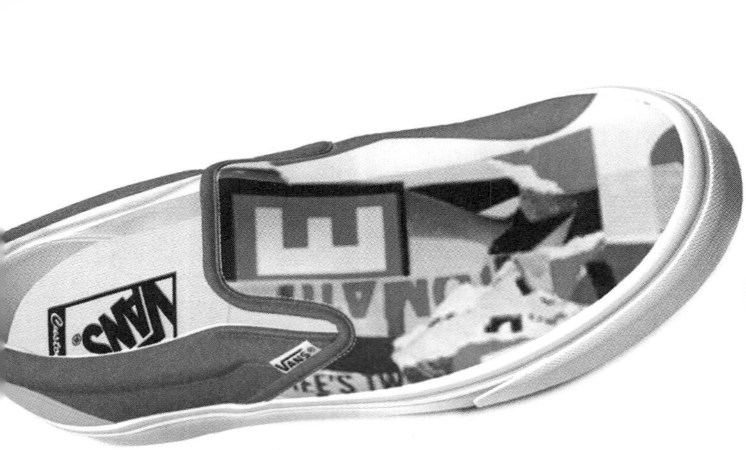
VANS

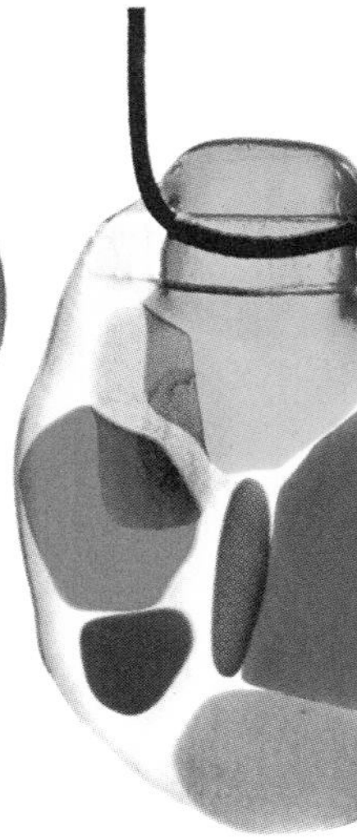

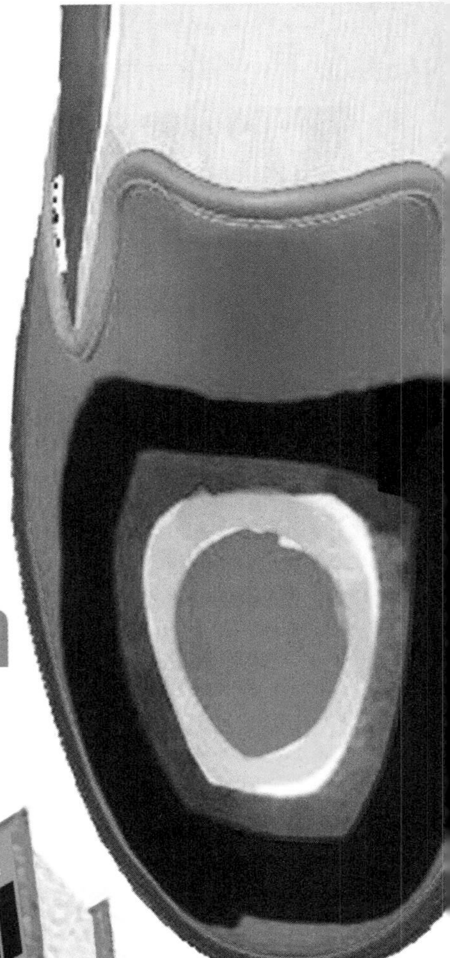

visit www.rosenworld.com

for

Sneakers, Signed Books,
Melty Jewels
and Original Artwork
by Laurie Rosenwald, First Pancake,
Occasional Swede
& America's
Favorite Bystander

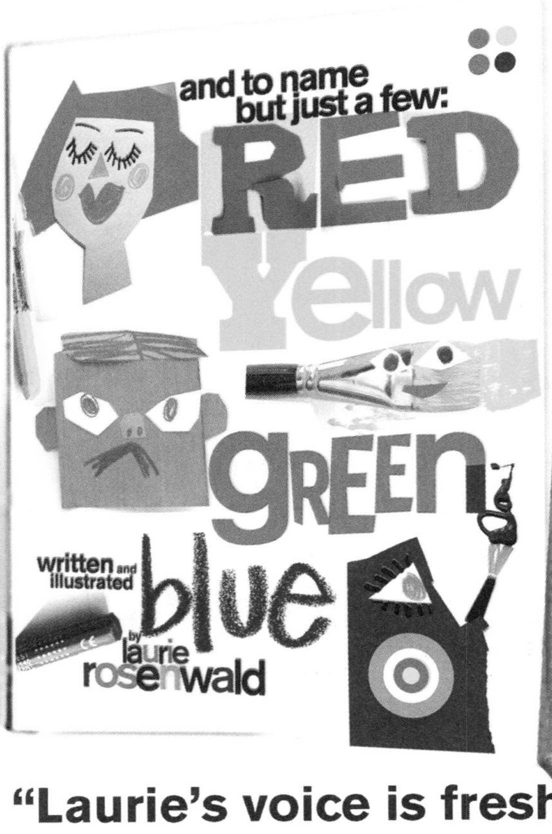
and to name but just a few:
RED
Yellow
GREEN
blue
written and illustrated by laurie rosenwald

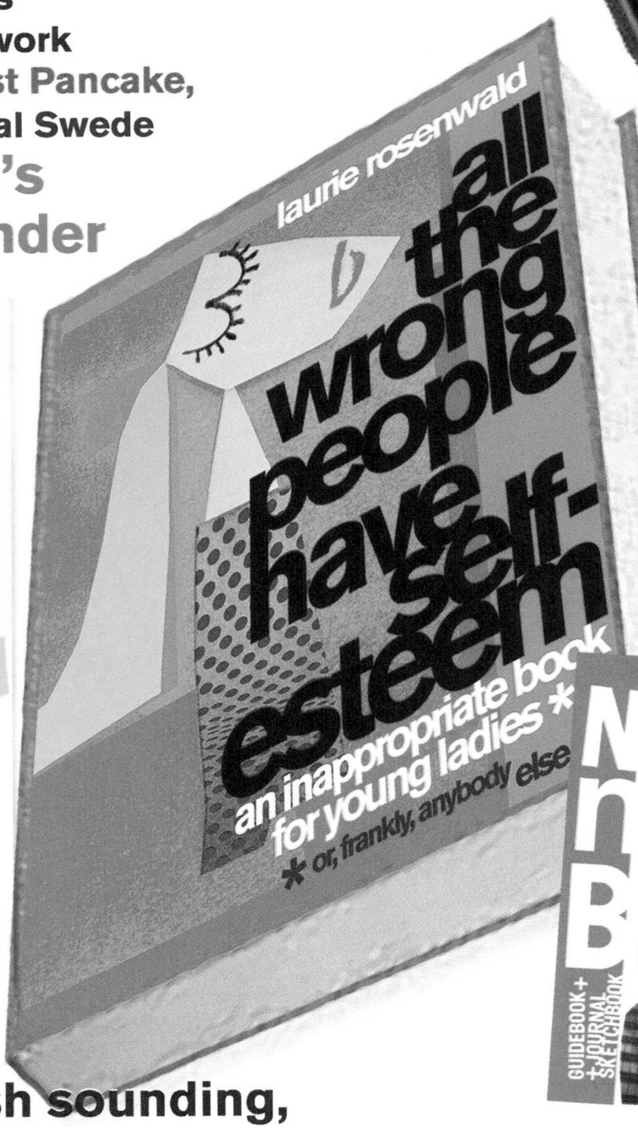
laurie rosenwald
all the wrong people have self-esteem
an inappropriate book for young ladies *
* or, frankly, anybody else

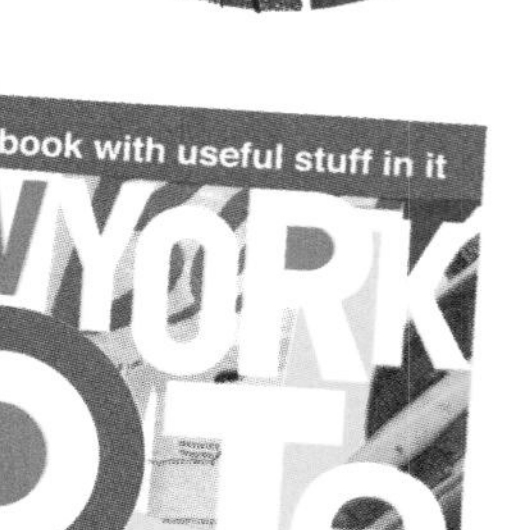

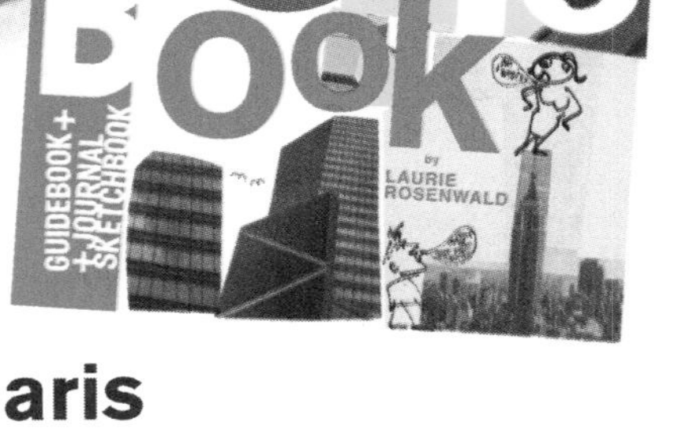
a blank book with useful stuff in it
NEW YORK noTe Book
GUIDEBOOK + JOURNAL + SKETCHBOOK
by LAURIE ROSENWALD

"Laurie's voice is fresh sounding, funny, and completely her own." -David Sedaris

WHAT AM I DOING HERE?

"The Happiest Country in South America"? Our Intrepid Traveler has notes. • ***By Mike Reiss***

You Go Uruguay, I'll Go Mine

It would be the worst Jan and Dean song ever: *"Four cows for every boy..."* But there truly are 3.8 cows for every person in Uruguay. And due to proximity (or perhaps inter-breeding), the Uruguayans are somewhat bovine: stocky, slow-moving, quiet and very contented. In fact, Uruguay has repeatedly been named "The Happiest Country in South America." I was skeptical—after all, Disneyland is called "The Happiest Place on Earth," and it's depressing and expensive and been home to eight accidental deaths and one murder.

My suspicions were aroused when we landed in the nation's capitol, Montevideo. It is the rare large city with no nice parts whatsoever. If we have a romantic vision of this place, it's because we mispronounce it with flair: "Monta-vi-DAY-o." The locals pronounce it "Monty Video," making it sound more like an '80s shop where a guy named Monty rents VHS tapes. Mostly porn.

The city is bisected by a pedestrian mall that extends for miles—but I never saw any pedestrians because it wasn't much of a mall: no restaurants, no shops, no video rental...just shuttered storefronts, graffiti, and bird crap. So much bird crap. At the end of the mall, I saw two homeless men cooking a steak over a cinderblock stuffed with newspaper. Uruguayans are the MacGyvers of grilling—they can fashion a barbecue out of anything: a broken bottle, a postage stamp, a block of ice. One of the dust-caked men offered me a hunk of their meat wrapped in a kitchen sponge. I took it—again, there were no restaurants around—and it was the greatest steak I ever ate in my life. And not great in the sense that "these poor men shared their meager meal with a total stranger in an act of true Christian charity." No—this was just a great-ass steak! When the cows outnumber the people four to one, there's no excuse for bad beef.

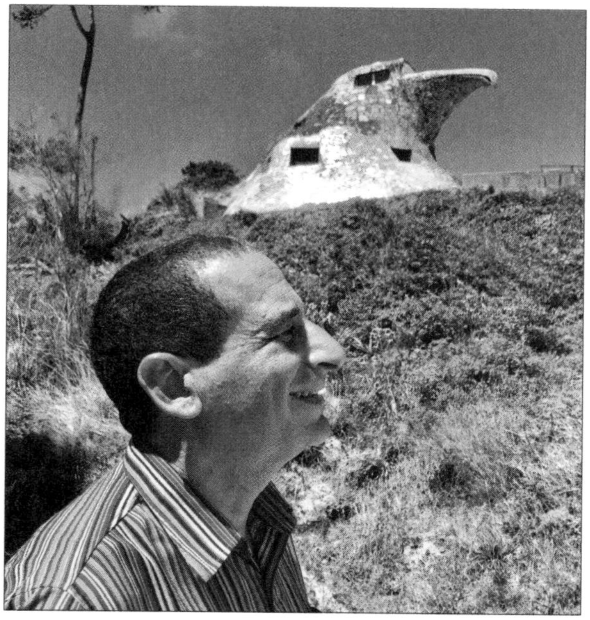

DENISE REISS

SEE, IT LOOKS LIKE AN EAGLE: *Mike posing in Atlantida, Uruguay, a city comprised entirely of quirk.*

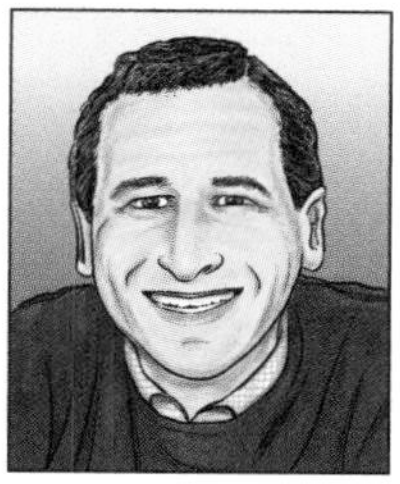

MIKE REISS is Intrepid Traveler for *The American Bystander*.

Steak is the main ingredient in the country's national dish, the *chivito*. It's a sandwich on French bread stuffed with an entire friggin' steak, as well as mozzarella, tomatoes, mayonnaise, black olives, green olives and bacon. Oh, and ham, too—that's right, it's got two kinds of pork. And in case all that doesn't kill you, it's topped with a fried egg. It's a sandwich designed by committee—everyone in Uruguay chose an ingredient, and all of them went in. The finished *chivito* is about the size of a piece of carry-on luggage, and costs around three bucks. That includes a side of fries so huge, it seems they've brought you every French fry on earth. The *chivito* is sold everywhere, from drugstores to fine restaurants, and everyone eats them completely—I watched small children devour sandwiches larger than themselves.

The locals wash down this Tyrannosandwich Rex with a drink just as unique: *mata*. Every Uruguayan walks the streets encumbered with a pouch of mata leaves, a thermos filled with hot water, a coconut-shaped drinking vessel, and a silver drinking straw...and generally a ringing cell phone and a crying infant. *Mata* looks like tea, has the kick of coffee, and is as complex to prepare as crystal meth. You pack the leaves in the coconut, pour a splash of hot water over it, and sip it slowly over the course of the day. I liked the stuff so much, I brought home a whole *mata* rig and five pounds of leaves. Months later, it sits unopened in my cupboard.

The number one tourist destination in Uruguay is Punta del Este, a spit of land that curls into the Atlantic, and comes to a point so sharp you could cut a *chivito* with it. Both sides of the peninsula are developed with high-rise beach resorts, but there's a catch: on the sheltered bay side, the weather is calm and warm; on the ocean side, you're perpetually battered by cold ocean winds. Can you guess which side Mr. Trump built his luxury condos? Here's a hint: the sign featuring Don Jr. in a construction hat has blown down and splintered to bits. You have to wonder about the quality of the condo construction when even the billboard can't stay up.

On the town's main beach stands the symbol of Punta del Este: a sculpture of five greenish fingers, each the size of a man, clawing their way out of the sand. What does it even mean? "Come for a

day at the beach…and get crushed by a giant from Hell!" I left town via the only bridge—it has four, huge, nausea-inducing humps in it for no good reason—and headed to Atlantida, a city comprised entirely of quirk. I passed by a house that looks like an eagle, a hotel that looks like a ship, and a church that looks like an army of ice cream cones—all within a mile. They weren't tourist attractions—they weren't even marked. I also visited the ruins of a castle that was inhabited by an alchemist… in 1966. Yes, Atlantida had a guy making a good living at alchemy there in the mid-1960s.

I reached my quirk quota, and then some, at a Uruguayan boutique hotel. It had no room numbers, just an abstract symbol on each door. This is fine until you get lost, which I did almost immediately. I spent three hours roaming the halls—was I in Zigzag or Squiggle? Spiral or Counterclockwise Spiral?

When I finally found my room, it was so crammed with idiosyncratic knicknacks, there was no place for my bags. "Where can I put my luggage?" I asked the manager.

"*Lug-gage*?" he asked. Forty years in the hotel business and he'd never encountered this concept.

I'd had enough. I wanted to go home to New York, where my house was shaped like a house and the number on the door was a number. This place was nice for awhile, but I finally got sick of its cuteness.

Just like Disneyland.

Nobody promised me Uruguay would be beautiful, or exciting or fascinating. They didn't even say I'd be happy there—just that the locals were. I didn't quite get this till I met the happiest man in New York. He wasn't a mayor or a mogul or a movie star—he was a shabby guy on the subway gibbering gleefully on his cell phone: "I'm just swimming along, singing a song! Got a couple of lampreys hanging off my belly and some barnacles on my tail. But life is good, man! Life. Is. Good!"

It took me a moment to realize three things about this guy:

1. *His cell phone was a baby shoe.*
2. *He thought he was a whale.*
3. *He was proud to be a whale, even if he really wasn't one.*

Uruguay is like that. It's a nation of four million kooks who are inordinately proud of their country for no good reason. They're proud of their *bizcochos*, the national dessert that's just salty crumbs held together with grease. And they choke these down with their local coffee, which may be the worst in the world. They've built gorgeous museums honoring their two best-known painters no one has ever heard of: Joaquin Torres Garcia (who draws like a child who owns four crayons) and Carlos Paez Villaro (who draws like Joaquin Torres Garcia). Uruguay really was a nice place to visit if you just lowered your standards enough.

Just like Disneyland.

That's the explanation I choose to believe, but there is a darker one. I asked a local man why Uruguay was so happy. "We have a stable government, a good economy and lower unemployment than our neighbors," he replied.

"And why is that?" I asked.

"I'm not proud of this—" he said, the only time I heard a local say that, "but in 1908 we killed or expelled all the poor people."

Again, just like Disneyl—nah, that's a cheap shot. **B**

P.S. MUELLER THINKS LIKE THIS

The cartoonist/broadcaster/writer is always walking around, looking at stuff • **By P.S. Mueller**

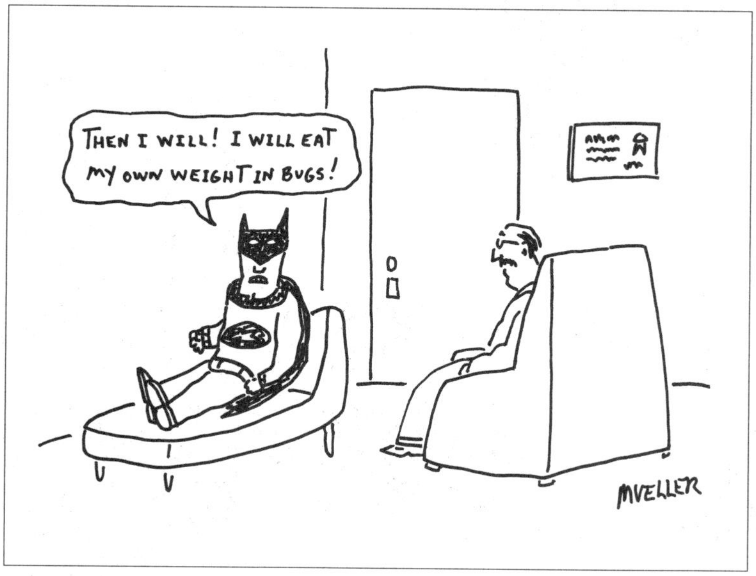
THEN I WILL! I WILL EAT MY OWN WEIGHT IN BUGS!
MUELLER

Prison Tips

• ***A metal cup.*** You need one of those to drag back and forth across the bars of your cell.
• ***Puppets.*** Trust me, you will NEED puppets.
• ***His name is Gorgox*** and he sleeps, if you can call that moist and wheezy crackle sleep, on the lower bunk. Do not attempt to bargain.
• ***Some guy*** has a tattoo of Roger Stone on his back.
• ***Stock up on shivs*** and pruno and work on the twisted grin.
• ***Before you go in***, have your arms surgically removed so you can say, "You should see the other guy," while leaning in to the dinner bowl.
• ***Remember jerky.*** The puppets won't forget.
• ***That rusty nail*** in the cement wall has been pried at by 24 inmates before you. Give it the old five-to-seven try.
• ***Nobody likes a rat***, especially a highly intelligent, seriously mutated and argumentative rat.
• ***When Day-Glo Chubby*** moves in, don't let him build imaginary golf courses.

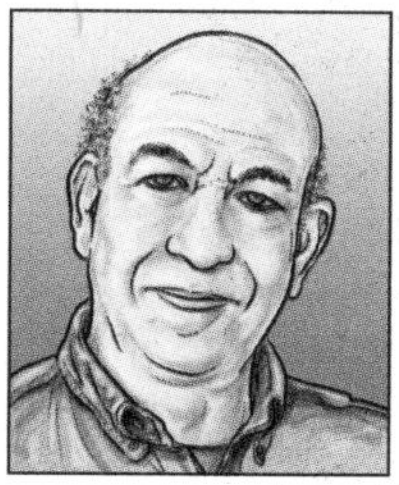

P.S. MUELLER is Staff Liar of *The American Bystander*.

Truly Incredible Nebber

Nebber began pushing buttons at an early age during the days before touchscreen technology. At age 23 Nebber was employed at some kind of internet startup and pushed a button, randomly producing an algorithmic patch that led to the dawn and day of online commerce. By 30 Nebber was worth seven billion dollars.

Nebber didn't know a thing about computers and programming; he was simply swept into a frantic new industry and had been faking everything because the money was great and no one cared what he did. So, immediately upon cashing in, Nebber built a palatial home in Rockford, Illinois, and went to live there. "Why Rockford?" people asked. After tiring of this, he gave each citizen of Rockford a million dollars to shut the fuck up.

Then everybody in Rockford left Rockford and Nebber was alone, except for his faithful pug dog Judy. Together, Nebber and Judy walked the vacant streets of a once-thriving city for a year. Up and down and around it they went, always keeping an eye out when the sun got low, because that's when the Dummlers came out.

The Dummlers were the one stubborn clan to remain, far too stubborn to follow the Rockford diaspora to Belvidere. The Dummlers lived in a natural shelter beneath a rock outcropping. For generations the Dummlers chipped and carved a remarkable estate into the large hill above them. Also, the Dummlers never accepted Nebber's money and insisted on asking "Why Rockford?" whenever he ran into them.

Otherwise, the Dummlers were peaceful folks, and every bit as wealthy as Nebber. No one knows how they acquired all that money, but some say they still receive royalties for the invention of fire. Nebber and the Dummlers simply lived apart and otherwise alone in a slowly unraveling city resembling something spat out of Wisconsin.

Judy the pug dog was along for the ride and having a ball. Nebber thought out loud in front of her and she learned to comprehend the rich nuance of the English language. She learned to read and type. And she pawed at Nebber's keyboard for two years, feverishly setting down the story of the greatest guy who ever lived, The Almighty Nebber. The Dummlers are not so, well, — actually, they're really nice and fun, but really—What in this tiny life could be better than Nebber? **B**

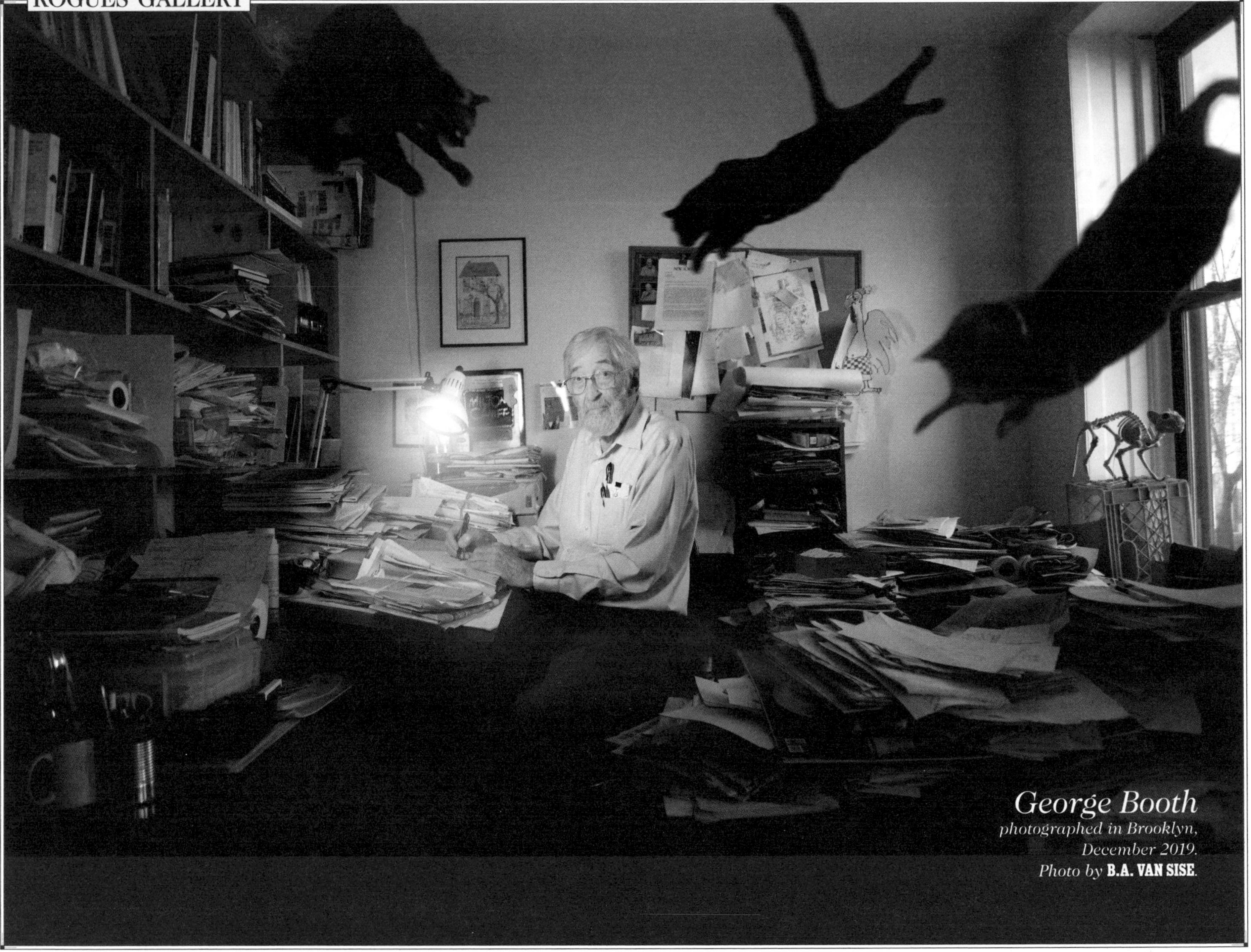

George Booth
photographed in Brooklyn, December 2019.
Photo by **B.A. VAN SISE**.